The
REVELATION

*An analysis and exposition
of the last book of the Bible*

by

ARNO C. GAEBELEIN

LOIZEAUX BROTHERS
Neptune, New Jersey

PUBLISHED 1961 by LOIZEAUX BROTHERS, Inc.

*A Nonprofit Organization, Devoted to the Lord's Work
and to the Spread of His Truth*

(Originally published by Our Hope Press)

Library of Congress Catalog Card Number   61-17225

PUBLISHED 1961 by LOIZEAUX BROTHERS, Inc.

CONTENTS

To my Beloved Wife

"Emma"

In appreciation of her prayers and sacrifices, which have been for many years a constant encouragement and cheer, as well as a help, in a busy life of service for God, this volume is affectionately dedicated.

THE REVELATION*

"The Revelation of Jesus Christ, which God gave unto Him—." This is the first sentence with which this last book in God's Word begins. The best title therefore is, "The Revelation of Jesus Christ." Our Lord received, according to this opening statement, a revelation from God. This must be understood in connection with Himself as the Son of Man. As the Only Begotten He had no need of a revelation; in His Deity He is acquainted with all the eternal purposes. One with God He knows the end from the beginning. But He, who is very God, took on in incarnation the form of a servant, and thus being in fashion as a man, He humbled Himself (Phil. ii: 7-8). And as the Man who had passed through death, whom God raised from the dead, and exalted at His own right hand, God gave Him this revelation concerning the judgment of the earth and the glory of Himself. "God raised Him from the dead and gave Him glory" (1 Peter i: 21). What this Glory is which He received from God is fully and blessedly revealed in this book. It is the revelation of His acquired Glory and how this Glory is to be manifested in connection with the earth. And this revelation He makes known to His servants, because His own are sharers with Him in all He received from God.

---

* Read this introduction several times before taking up the study of the book.

Pre-eminently His Revelation

The Revelation is pre-eminently His revelation; the revelation of His Person and His Glory. "In the volume of the book it is written of Me....." (Heb. x:7). Martin Luther asked, "What Book and what Person?" and answered, "There is only one Book— the Bible; and only one Person—Jesus Christ." The whole Book, the Word of God, bears witness of Him, Who is the living Word. He is the center, the sum total and the substance of the Holy Scriptures. The prayerful reader of the Bible will never read in vain if he approaches the blessed Book with the one desire to know Christ and His Glory. His blessed face is seen on every page and the infallible Guide, the Holy Spirit, never fails to satisfy the longing of the believer's heart to know more of Christ. Inasmuch as this last Bible book is the Revelation of Jesus Christ, an "Unveiling" of Himself, we find in it the completest revelation of His Person and His Glory.

It is here where many expositions of Revelation have missed the mark. Occupied chiefly with the symbols of the Book, the mysteries, the judgments and the promised consummation. they have neglected to emphasize sufficiently Him, who throughout this Book is pre-eminently the center of everything. The reader of Revelation does well to read first of all through the entire Book with this object in mind, to see what is said of our Lord, of His Person, His present and His future Glory.

We shall find all the features of His Person and His Work mentioned. He is the Alpha and Omega,

the first and the last (i: 11); the Ancient of Days
(i: 14 compare with Daniel vii: 9); the "I Am,"
that is, Jehovah, "I am He that liveth" (i: 18); the
Son of God (ii: 18). These terms speak of His Deity.
His earthly life in humiliation is touched upon in the
statement, "the faithful Witness" (i: 5). His death
on the cross is likewise mentioned—"He hath washed
us from our sins in His blood" (i: 5); "He was dead"
(i: 18); "the Lamb as it had been slain" (v: 6);
"worthy is the Lamb that was slain" (v: 12). He is
mentioned twenty-eight times as the Lamb in Revelation and each time it reminds us of the cross and the
great work accomplished there. His resurrection is
seen, for He is called, "the First begotten from the
dead" (i: 5), and He speaks of Himself as, "He that
was dead, and, behold, I am alive forevermore" (i: 18);
and again, "these things saith the first and the last,
who was dead and is alive" (ii: 8).

Then we behold Him "in the midst" in glory, seen
face to face by all the redeemed and worshipped by
them, as well as by the heavenly hosts and ultimately
by every creature, the fulfillment of Phil. ii: 10-11,
"that at the name of Jesus every knee should bow,
of things in heaven, and things on earth and things
under the earth, and that every tongue should confess
that Jesus Christ is Lord, to the glory of God the
Father" (Rev. v: 18-14). After the fifth chapter we
have His revelation as the executor of the decreed
judgments. He opens the seals; He sends forth the
seven angels with the judgment trumpets and the seven
angels with the judgment vials, in which the wrath of

God is completed. "The Father judgeth no man, but has committed all judgment unto the Son" (John v: 22). Then He is seen in the glorious union with the Bride (xix: 7-10) and as the victorious Christ who passeth out of heaven followed by the armies of heaven (xix: 11-21), conquering the opposing forces of evil, executing the wrath of Almighty God, appearing as King of kings and Lord of lords. The twentieth chapter reveals Him as the reigning Christ. He and His Saints with Him will reign over the earth for a thousand years. And all which follows reveals Him and His Glory as well as the blessed and eternal results of His work.

A Book of Prophecy

Aside from the title of the Book, which indicates that it deals with things future, there is a direct statement which determines its prophetic character. In the first beatitude of the seven which are found in the Book, we read that it is a Book of Prophecy— "Blessed is he that readeth, and they that hear the words of this Prophecy" (i: 3). It is known to every intelligent student of the Bible that a good part of it is Prophecy. The great prophecies concerning the people Israel and the nations of the world are found in the Old Testament Scriptures. In the New Testament there is but one Book of Prophecy, the Revelation. As it is the capstone of the entire revelation of God, without which the Bible would be an unfinished book, we find in its pages the consummation of the great Prophecies which were given by the Prophets of God in Old Testament times.

For the study of this New Testament Prophetic
Book the knowledge of the chief content of the Old
Testament Prophetic Word is therefore an absolute
necessity. For instance to a Christian who does not
have a fair grasp of Daniel's great Prophecies, or is
ignorant of the place which the people Israel hold
in the purposes of God, the Book of Revelation is a
sealed book, without any possible meaning. This is
one of the chief reasons why this Book has suffered
so much both from the critics and from the hands of
commentators. The Apostle Peter saith, "Knowing
this first, that no prophecy of the Scripture is of any
private interpretation. For the prophecy came not
in old time by the will of man, but holy men of God
spake as they were moved by the Holy Spirit" (2 Peter
i: 20-21). The better translation for "private interpretation" is, "its own interpretation." It means that
the interpretation of prophecy must be done by com-
paring Scripture with Scripture. The holy men of
God, the prophets, were the instruments of the Holy
Spirit and made known God's purposes in a progres-
sive way. To understand any prophecy is only possible
by taking the entire Prophetic Word into consideration. That there is a wonderful harmony in the great
body of prophetic dispensational truths as found in
the Bible we have demonstrated in another volume. *
This principle finds its strongest application in the interpretation of the Revelation.

---

*"Harmony of the Prophetic Word"—a volume which has
been used under God's blessing to open the minds of many
to the meaning of Prophecy.

The Three Classes

In I Corinthians x:32 the Apostle Paul speaks of three classes into which the human race is divided: the Jews, the Gentiles, and the Church of God. In the Old Testament there was no Church of God, for the Church is a New Testament institution. As the Revelation is the book of consummation these three classes must be seen in the contents of this Book. Many expositors have seen nothing but the struggles of the Church in her history in this Book. This is true of the so-called Preterist school and also of the Historical school of interpretation. The Preterist school teaches a fulfillment of all the apocalyptic visions in the struggles of the Church in the past. The Historical school also teaches that the visions concern mostly the Church. These schools of interpretation leave out the Jews and what is written concerning them and their final history during the end of the age, preceding the glorious appearing of our Lord. Of late another school of interpreters has come into existence. They teach that the entire Book of Revelation concerns the Jewish people and that there is nothing about the Church in this last Book of the Bible. Any interpretation of Revelation which ignores the Jews, the people Israel and the fulfillment of Old Testament predictions concerning them is wrong. And any interpretation which teaches that there is nothing about the Church in Revelation is equally wrong. The Church and her destiny on earth, the destiny of the true Church and the destiny of the apostate Church, or Christendom, is found in the Book. The Jews and what concerns them in the end of the age, the Gentiles, the nations of the earth, and the judgments in store for them, as well as the future of the earth, a future of glory and blessing; all this is found in our New Testament Book of Prophecy.

The True Interpretation

There is a true interpretation of Revelation which is in harmony with all previous prophecies and which opens the Book to our understanding. But how are we to find this true interpretation? We answer, the Book itself furnishes it. This is an important fact, both convincing and conclusive. It is therefore of no profit to examine the different theories and schools of interpretation. We shall avoid the terms Preterist, Historical and Futurist, and not try, as it has been attempted, to reconcile these different modes of interpretation. There must be one true interpretation, and we claim that this is given to us by the Lord Himself in this Book.

The Key Which Fits

It has often been truthfully said, every Book in the Bible contains a key which unlocks the Book. The Revelation is no exception. John the beloved disciple was in banishment in the isle of Patmos, as Daniel the man greatly beloved, was a captive in Babylon. The Lord called these two great servants to behold the panorama of the future. Both wrote down their visions. While in the Book of Daniel we find no direct command to write, we find such a command in the first chapter of Revelation. John received

divine instruction how to write the Revelation. We
find this in the nineteenth verse, "Write therefore
what thou hast seen, and the things that are, and the
things that are about to be after these." * John,
guided by the Holy Spirit then wrote the Revelation
according to the divine direction. In examining this
command to write we find that three things are mentioned. He is to write first the things he had seen.
then the things which are, and finally the things that
are about to be after these. When John received
these instructions he had already seen something, and
the vision he had he was instructed to write down.
Then present things, the things which are, and future
things, to be after present things have passed away,
must be located in this book. So we have the past,
the present and the future in this key verse.

Three Divisions—Where are They?

It is then clear that the Book of Revelation must be
divided into three main divisions. How are we to
locate these divisions? They are marked, so that we
are not left in doubt about it. In the beginning of
the fourth chapter we find a significant statement
which shows where the third division begins. After
these things, that is after the contents of the opening
three chapters were past, John heard the same voice
speaking to him once more. He sees a door opened
in heaven and is told, "Come up hither, and I will
shew thee the things which must take place after these
things" (iv: 1). There can then be no doubt at all

---

* This is the correct translation of this important verse.

that with the fourth chapter the seer beheld the things which take place after the preceding things, the things which are, have passed away. The third division of Revelation begins with the fourth chapter. John beholds future things from heaven into which he had been taken "in the Spirit." The things he had seen and the things which are, are therefore contained in the first three chapters of the Book.

The first chapter contains the things he had seen. "What thou seest write in a book" was the first instruction John received (verse 11). In the nineteenth verse he is told, "Write therefore what thou hast seen." Between verse 11 and verse 19 he saw a vision, which he was to write, and this vision constitutes the first section or division of the Book. The second and third chapters form the second division, the things which are. The beginning of the fourth chapter to the end of the Book is the final, the third division. There is no better and more logical key. And this key given in the Book determines the true interpretation.

The Patmos Vision

"The things thou hast seen"—the first section of Revelation is the great Patmos vision, chapter i: 12-18. It is the vision of the glorified Son of Man in the midst of the seven golden candlesticks (or lampstands).

The Things Which Are

The things which are, the present things, begin the prophetic section of the Revelation. The second and third chapters of Revelation, the things which are, contain the messages of our Lord addressed to the seven churches of Asia Minor. These messages contain the first great Prophecy of Revelation. The prophecy concerns the Church on earth. We shall show in our comment on these two chapters that we have in them a divine history of the Church on earth. It is one of the most remarkable sections of the Prophetic Word. What this present age is to be religiously and how it will end is made known in other parts of the New Testament. Our Lord in some of His Kingdom parables (Matthew xiii) reveals the characteristics of this age. The parables of the sower, the evil seed sown into the field, the mustard seed parable and the parable of the leaven are prophetic and teach, in part at least, what the church messages reveal. The Holy Spirit in the Epistolar testimony also reveals the religious and moral characteristics of the age, and depicts its departure from the truth, and its end. The destiny of the true Church is heavenly. She has a "blessed hope," which is to be with the Lord in Glory. She is the Body of Christ, and He is the "Head of the Body." The Church is also the Bride of Christ and He is the Bridegroom. The Body is united to the Head in Glory; the Bride will be joined to the Bridegroom. 1 Thessalonians iv: 13-18 is the Scripture which reveals this end for the true Church on earth. The professing Church, Christendom, which rejects the doctrine of Christ and goes into apostasy has a far different destiny. The Lord will disown that which hath denied His Name, and judgment and wrath is to be poured out upon apostate Christendom (2 Thess. i: 7-9). These predictions concerning the Church on earth are contained in the seven church messages. When we come to the close of the third chapter we find a significant promise, and equally significant threat. "I also will keep thee from the hour of temptation (trial) which shall come upon all the world, to try them that dwell upon the earth" (iii: 10). This is the promise. It tells of the removal of the true Church, composed of all true believers, from this earthly scene. "I will spue thee out of my mouth" (iii: 6). This is the threat to the apostate Church. Both the promise and the threat will be fulfilled. After the third chapter the word church does not occur again in Revelation. The reason for this is obvious. The history of the Church on earth terminates with the close of the third chapter. Because the true Church is no longer here but has been taken up into Glory, and that which professes to be the Church is disowned by the Lord, therefore no more mention of the Church is made in Revelation.

The Things Which Are After These

The future things, things after the removal of the true Church from the earth, occupy the greater part of this Book. It is of the greatest importance to see that nothing whatever after the third chapter of Revelation has yet taken place. Some speak of a past and partial fulfillment of some of the visions found in this section. In view of the scope of the Book this is impossible. The open door in heaven, the voice which calls the seer to pass through that open door into heaven, is symbolical of the great coming event, the realization of the blessed Hope of the coming of the Lord for His Saints. That this open door

is mentioned immediately after the third chapter and
John is suddenly in the spirit in the presence of the
throne in heaven is very significant. It proves that
the entire situation is now changed. And the first
great vision is a vision of the Saints in Glory, occupying thrones and worshipping God and the Lamb. With
the sixth chapter the great judgment visions of this
Book begin. These great punitive dealings with the
earth are executed from above. All transpires after
the Lord has taken His Saints into Glory. No seal
can be broken as long as this event has not been.
But after the Rapture, the Seals of the Book, which
the Lamb received, are broken by Him, the trumpet
and the vial judgments fall upon the earth. All this
takes place after the home-going of the true Church
and before the glorious appearing of our Lord Jesus
Christ (xix: 11, etc.).

Now this portion of Revelation from chapter vi
to xix contains the events which transpire during the
end of the age. It is the unfulfilled seventieth week
of the great prophecy in the Book of Daniel (Dan.
ix: 24-27). This "end of the age" will last twice
1260 days, that is seven years. It is absolutely necessary to understand the scope of the seventy-week
prophecy in Daniel in order to understand the greater
part of these chapters in the Revelation.* We are led
back upon Jewish ground. Events in connection with
the Jewish people and Jerusalem are before us. The
times of the Gentiles have taken on their final form

---

* "The Prophet Daniel" by A. C. G. contains a very simple
exegesis of Daniel's prophecies.

of ten kingdoms which Daniel saw on the fourth beast
as ten horns, and Nebuchadnezzar on the image as
ten toes.   The empire in which these ten Kingdoms
come into existence.is the Roman empire.   It will
have a revival and come into existence again.   Then
a wicked leader will take the headship of that resurrected Roman empire, and another Beast, the false
prophet, the Anti-christ will domineer over the Jewish
people and persecute their saints, the remnant of
Israel, while the earth and the dwellers upon the earth
experience the great judgments.   The last half of
these seven years is called the great tribulation.   We
must also remember that our Lord left behind a great
Prophecy concerning the end of the age.   This
Prophecy is contained in the Olivet Discourse, the
first part of which (Matt. xxiv: 4-44) harmonizes in
a striking manner with the events in Revelation vi-xix.
Our Lord calls special attention to Daniel and likewise
speaks of the great tribulation.   In our brief exposition we shall point out some of the interesting and
convincing details.

The glorious climax is the visible manifestation of
the Lord out of heaven, crowned with many crowns,*
the defeat and overthrow of the Beast and the kings
of the earth and their armies, the binding of Satan,
and the reign of Christ with His Saints for a thousand years.   After that follows the great white throne
judgment, which is the judgment of the wicked dead,
the glories of the new Jerusalem, the eternal destiny
of the redeemed and the eternal destiny of the lost.

---

* Compare Revelation xix: 11-21 with Daniel vii: 11-14 and
Matthew xxiv: 27-31.

If this last great Book of the Bible is studied in this divinely given order it will no longer be, as is so often said, a sealed book. All fanciful interpretations and applications of these great visions to past or present history can no longer be maintained as soon as we reckon with the fact that these visions are not yet fulfilled, and are going to be fulfilled after the true Church is no longer on the earth.

The Promised Blessing

"Blessed is he that readeth, and they that hear the words of this Prophecy, and keep those things which are written therein, for the time is at hand" (verse 3). A blessing is promised to him who readeth, and who hears and keeps. It does not say that a blessing is for him who understands and knows everything which is in this Book. If such were the condition the writer and the reader would have no claim on this promised blessing. The Bible-teacher, or any other man, who says he knows and understands everything found in this great finale of God's Word is very much mistaken. We cannot be sure about everything in some of these visions and the full meaning of some may not be understood till the world sees the fulfillment. The blessing is promised to all His people who give attention to the Revelation of Jesus Christ. What is the blessing we may expect through the reading and prayerful study of the words of this Prophecy?

First of all we receive through this Book a wonderful vision of our Saviour and Lord. This is what we

need as His people above everything else, and it is
this which brings blessing into our lives. As stated
before, this Book is pre-eminently His revelation, a
blessed unveiling of His person and Glory. But we
also get another blessing. In reading through this
Book we see what is in store for this age, what judgments will overtake the world, and how Satan's power
will be manifested to the full upon those who rejected
His grace. Judgment, tribulation and wrath are
swiftly coming upon this age. Out of all this our
gracious Lord has delivered us. There is no judgment, no wrath for us who know Him as our sin-bearer
and our hiding-place. Praise must fill our hearts when
we read the words of this Prophecy and remember
the grace which has saved us from all which is coming upon this age. Another blessing is the assurance
of ultimate victory and glory. Dark is the age, and
becoming darker, but in Revelation we behold the
glory which is coming for His Saints first of all and
after the judgment clouds are gone, for Jerusalem, the
nations and the earth. Reading Revelation fills the
heart with the assurance and certainty of the outcome of all. It is a solemn atmosphere which fills the
whole Book of Revelation. As we continue to read
and continue to breathe this heavenly and solemn atmosphere it will result in a closer walk with God, a
more spiritual worship and a greater and more unselfish service for Him "Who loveth us and hath
washed us from our sins in His own blood, and hath
made us priests and kings unto God His Father."

THE ANALYSIS OF THE REVELATION.

Title: The Revelation of Jesus Christ.

I. THE PATMOS VISION OF THE GLORIFIED SON OF MAN. CHAPTER I.

1. The Book, its title and introduction. Verses 1-3.
2. Greeting and Benediction. Verses 4-5.
3. The Outburst of Praise. Verses 6-7.
4. The Testimony of the Almighty. Verse 8.
5. John in Patmos. Verses 9-11.
6. The Great Vision of the Son of Man in **Glory.** Verses 12-16.
7. The Effect and the Commission. Verses 17-21.

II. THE THINGS WHICH ARE. THE SEVEN CHURCH MESSAGES REVEALING THE HISTORY OF THE CHURCH ON EARTH. CHAPTERS II-III.

CHAPTER II.

1. Ephesus, the Post-Apostolic Period. Verses 1-7.
2. Smyrna, the Period of Persecution. Verses 8-11.
3. Pergamos, the Period of Corruption. Verses 12-17.
4. Thyatira, the Romish Corruption. Verses 18-29.

CHAPTER III.

5. Sardis, the Reformation Period. Verses 1-6.
6. Philadelphia, the Faithful Remnant. Verses 7-13.
7. Laodicea, the Indifferent and Apostate **Church.** Verses 14-22.

Between the Sixth and Seventh Seal. A Parenthetical Vision. (Chapter VII.)

CHAPTER VII.

    1. The Remnant of Israel Called and Sealed. Verses 1-8.

    2. The Saved Multitude of Gentiles Coming out of the Great Tribulation. Verses 9-17.

        End of the Parenthesis.

    3. The Seventh Seal. Verses 1-5.

CHAPTER VIII: 1-5.

Third Division: The Sounding of the Seven Trumpets. Chapters VIII: 6-XI: 18.

CHAPTER VIII: 6-13.

    1. The First Trumpet. Verses 6-7.

    2. The Second Trumpet. Verses 8-9.

    3. The Third Trumpet. Verses 10-11.

    4. The Fourth Trumpet. Verses 12-13.

CHAPTER IX.

    5. The Fifth Trumpet. The First Woe. Verses 1-12.

    6. The Sixth Trumpet. The Second Woe. Verses 13-21.

Between the Sixth and Seventh Trumpets. Parenthetical Visions. (Chapters X-XI: 14.)

CHAPTER X.

    1. The Descending Angel. Verses 1-7.

    2. The Little Book. Verses 8-11.

CHAPTER XI.

    3. The Temple, Altar and Jewish Worshippers. Verses 1-2.

    4. The Two Witnesses. Verses 3-6.

    5. The Beast and the Witnesses. Verse 7.

    6. The Treatment of the Slain Witnesses. Verses 8-10.

    7. Their Public Vindication. Verses 11-12.

EXEGETICAL ANNOTATIONS

I. The Patmos Vision of the Glorified Son of Man.

Chapter I

1. The Book: Its Title and Introduction. Verses 1-3. As we have already spoken of the title and the prophetic character of the book, we do not repeat it here. The book does not contain, as it is often said "revelations," but one great revelation and that the Revelation of Jesus Christ. And this revelation is "to show unto His servants things which must shortly come to pass," so that they may know the future and serve Him with the Glory-light thrown upon their path. The vision of the future is much needed as an incentive for true and devoted service.

2. Greeting and Benediction. Verses 4-5. The churches which John addressed were in the Province of Asia, not the continent Asia, but one of the provinces of Asia Minor. (See Acts xvi: 6; xix: 10, etc.). These seven churches are representatives of the entire church, and prophetically unfold the history of the church on earth. "Grace unto you and Peace" is the greeting. Grace and peace are the blessed possessions of the true children of God. Though the professing church may fail in her testimony, and the dark days of apostasy increase, grace and peace for God's servants and children will never fail. The greeting differs from those found in the Epistles. In the Epistles the greetings come from the Father and the Son; the Holy Spirit being omitted. Here Jehovah is mentioned first, "who is, who was and who is to come"—"the I Am that I am"—the Self-existing One (Ex. iii: 14). Then comes the Holy Spirit, spoken of here as "the seven Spirits." Not as the "one Spirit" (Eph. iv: 4; 1 Cor. xii: 13) is He mentioned, but in His own complete fullness and His diverse activities (Isaiah xi: 2). And finally the name of our Lord Jesus Christ. "He is the faithful witness;" this describes His holy and perfect life on earth. "The first begotten from the dead." He died that shameful death on the cross and finished the Work the Father gave Him to do. Risen from the dead He is the first begotten as well as the first fruits. "The Prince of the kings of the earth." This is His future title and reveals His coming Glory. What comfort there is here for God's people! Oh, the grace and peace which flow from a believing contemplation of Himself and the knowledge that we are one with Him!

3. The Outburst of Praise. Verses 6-7. The last sentence of verse 5 belongs to verse 6. This inspired outburst of Praise is the true Glory song of the true Church. It contains the blessed fundamentals of the Gospel of Grace, what He has done for us and what He has made us and what we shall be with Him. It is the first doxology in this book. Others follow and increase in adoration. Twofold here; threefold in iv: 11; fourfold in v: 13; sevenfold in vii: 12. The tribute is followed by a testimony of His Coming. It is not His coming for His Saints but His coming to the earth. Compare with Acts i: 11; Matthew xxiv: 30; Daniel vii: 13; Zech. xii: 9-14.

4. *The Testimony of the Almighty. Verse 8.* **God,** so to speak, puts His seal to it all. The words of the preceding verse "Even so Amen" must be read with this verse. The speaker is Jehovah.

5. *John in Patmos. Verses 9-11.* John was in banishment in the isle of Patmos and "became in the Spirit on the Lord's day." Does this mean "the Day of the Lord" *i. e.* the day on which He comes in power and glory to begin His reign, or does it mean the blessed memorial day, the first day of the week? It means without doubt the latter.

6. *The Great Vision of the Glorified Son of Man. Verses 12-16.* John turned to see the voice. He beheld the greatest vision human eyes have seen. The seven golden candlesticks (lamp-stands) represent the seven churches (verse 20) and are symbolical of the entire church. He himself is "in the midst" and seen by John "like unto a Son of Man." But the vision makes it clear that He is more than a Son of Man, for He is the Ancient of Days as well. The title Son of Man belongs to Him both in His humiliation and exaltation. He was the Son of Man on earth; he is the Son of Man in Glory; and when He comes back to earth and receives the kingdom, it will be as Son of Man. Judgment will be executed by Him. In this vision His judicial character is the leading feature. He is clothed with a robe down to His feet. While this denotes priestly dignity we see Him not engaged in priestly activity. The long-robed figure expresses the great dignity of Himself as the Priest-King who is about to enter upon His work as Judge. The golden girdle is symbolical of **divine**

righteousness; His white head and hair identify Him with the Ancient of Days who sits in judgment (Daniel vii:9-12). The flaming eyes, all searching; the fiery burning feet; the voice like the sound of many waters (Psalm xxix); the two-edged sword; the face which was once marred and dishonored, now shining like the sun—all is symbolical and speaks of the great dignity and glory and the judicial rights of the Son of Man. His judgment in this book begins at the house of God, that which professes His Name; judgment is executed by Him on the earth and all culminates in His visible and glorious appearing, when all things will be put in subjection under His feet.

There is one feature of the vision which needs an explanation. What do the seven stars mean, which are in the right hand of the Son of Man? Verse 20 gives the answer. They are the seven angels of the seven churches. Angels and stars are symbolical figures. The application of these terms to church-officers or bishops and pastors is incorrect. Stars are used in Scripture to typify true believers. Stars are heavenly bodies which shine during the night; so are true believers in a heavenly position with the responsibility to shine in the night. The lamp-stands represent the visible, professing church; the stars represent the true believing element in the Church. They are in the right hand of Himself, held securely there. Furthermore, only true believers have an ear to hear what the Spirit saith. The stars are called angels, because an angel is a messenger and true believers are likewise that.

*7. The Effect of the Vision and the Commission.
Verses 17-20.* John fell at His feet as dead; the
vision was overpowering. Compare with Daniel
x:4-11. But He put His hand upon Him. Blessed is
His own testimony. He is the Living One, which
means "Jehovah." He was dead. And alive forevermore; He is risen from the dead and hath the keys
of Death and of Hades. Then follows the command
to write which we have fully explained in the introduction.

II. The Things Which Are. The Seven Church Messages Revealing the History of the Church on Earth

Chapters II and III

These two chapters are extremely rich in prophetic and spiritual truths. "The things which are," the second division of this book, is now before us. The churches mentioned in the two chapters, and never after, actually existed. They can easily be located geographically and traced historically. We do not attempt this as it has no spiritual value. These messages of course had a deep and significant meaning for the different local assemblies. That there are many spiritual lessons written in these messages, is also true. However, all this must take a secondary place. The primary thing is the prophetic interpretation. The seven churches represent the entire Church on earth, as already stated, and the conditions of these seven churches foreshadow the different periods of the Church on earth from the Apostolic times to the ending days, when the Lord calls His Saints to meet Him in the air. There were many hundreds of churches in existence throughout the countries where the Gospel had been preached. But messages from the Glorified Son of Man were not sent to all of them. Only seven, and these closely connected in the province of Asia, were selected by the Lord. The Son of Man is the omniscient Lord and as such He knows the end from the beginning. He knew the entire history of the Church from the beginning. He knew the coming persecutions, declensions, revivals, the perversions of His truth, the denials of His Name, the depths of Satan and the final apostasy. In the days of His humiliation that future was not hidden from Him, for in the Kingdom parables He revealed the religious conditions of this Christian age (Matthew xiii). With divine knowledge of what this age would bring forth and how it would end, He looked with His all-searching eyes into the condition of the different churches. He saw in seven of them conditions which were in embryo, the conditions through which the whole church on earth would pass, so that we have in these seven messages, which uncover the state of the different churches, the spiritual and religious history of Christendom. Our hints on all this must necessarily be brief, but enough will be given to prove the application.

1. Ephesus, the Apostolic and Post-Apostolic Period. Verses 1-7. Ephesus means "desired"; the Church is the object of His love, as is so beautifully stated in the Epistle to the Ephesians. He loved the Church and gave Himself for it; He cleanseth and sanctifieth it and He will present it to Himself a glorious Church (Ephes. v : 25-27). To that Church was communicated the highest revelation, especially the truth concerning the Church as the body and glory of Christ. Ephesus stands therefore for the first period of the Church on earth. The Lord bears witness to its faithfulness. For His Name's sake they labored and fainted not. What is especially a mark of the Apostolic and post-Apostolic times is the statement "thou hast tried or tested them which say they are apostles and are not,

and hast found them liars." Compare this with 2
Cor. xi: 13 "for such are false apostles, deceitful (lying) workers." Men arose who pretended to be
apostles even while the apostles were still living and
more so after their departure. But the early church
did not tolerate these false apostles who appeared in
large numbers during the second half of the first
century. The deeds of the Nicolaitanes they also
hated. What the Nicolaitanes were we shall find later.
But the Lord touches the sore spot, the beginning of
evil in the words "I have against thee because thou
hast left thy first love." What is the first love? The
Apostle Paul in his heart devotion to the Person of
Christ, with His burning desire to know Christ and
to win Christ, with His wonderful confession "Christ
is all in all"—"not I, but Christ," illustrates the first
love. The affection for Christ and devotion to Him,
the One altogether lovely, was waning. Outwardly
everything may have looked right, but the Lord, who
desires the deepest affection of His people, knew that
their hearts were departing from Him. This is the
starting point of all church and individual failure.
Their hearts were growing cold towards Himself.
Think it over! The beginning of evil, in doctrine or
in life, is heart-departure from Christ, and not giving
Christ the pre-eminence. Read also Paul's prediction
concerning Ephesus and what should come after his
departure (Acts xx: 29-30).

2. *Smyrna, the Period of Persecution. Verses 8-11.*
Smyrna stands for the next period up to about 313
A. D. Smyrna means "myrrh," which was one of the
ingredients of the perfume used for the embalming

of the dead. The Lord in addressing this church speaks of Himself as He "who was dead and is alive." It is the Church in tribulation and persecution. This is clearly marked in the message itself. "Behold the devil shall cast some of you into prison that ye may be tried; and ye shall have tribulation ten days; be thou faithful unto death and I will give thee a crown of life." Such a martyr-period is recorded in the history of the Church. The number ten is of special interest, for history informs us that there were just ten great persecutions of Christians by the Roman emperors. It was the work of the devil. Persecution of the Saints of God by pagan Rome, papal Rome or by any other power, is always the devil's work. But who are those mentioned here and in the message to Philadelphia, who say they are Jews and are not, but are of the synagogue of Satan? It is a Judaized Christianity and with it a perverted and obscured Gospel. That evil was present in the apostolic age; it is fully manifested in our own days. They deny the Gospel of Grace and put in its place the Gospel of works and salvation by character in keeping the law. They make much of Sabbath-keeping, ordinances and religious observances and yet with it all they obscure the Cross and deny the Blood. They are the synagogue of Satan, brought together by that cunning being as a religious company. It is the false, the spurious Church as we see it almost universally about us.

3. *Pergamos, the Period of Worldly Corruption. Verses 12-17.* Pergamos means "a thorough marriage." Pergamos is described as dwelling where

Satan's throne (not seat) is. And Satan's throne is not in Hell, but his throne is in the world, this present evil age, whose god he is (2 Cor. iv: 4). This shows prophetically that period when the church gave up her pilgrim character and was thoroughly married to the world. A great change took place. When the devil found that "the blood of the martyrs is the seed of the Church" he stopped his work as the roaring lion and took on the form of an angel of light. What had led to Israel's ruin was brought by the enemy into the professing Church, that is an unholy alliance with the world. The instrument used to accomplish this was the Emperor Constantine. The suffering, persecuted Church became joined to the world, wedded to the state; Constantine made the Church a world-institution. This third church-period corresponds to the third parable in Matthew xiii. The little mustard seed became a big tree, rooted in the field (the world) and the branches filled with birds (representing unconverted people). Church historians have spoken of Constantine's work as the work of God and a victory of Christianity. It was rather the opposite, the work of the enemy and the defeat of true Christianity. The name of Balaam appears also. When he could not curse Israel, he put the daughters of Midian and Moab amongst the people of God and in the unlawful mixture which followed he succeeded in hurting Israel (Numbers xxxi: 16; xxv: 1-2; Jude ii). And here the Nicolaitanes are mentioned for the second and last time. The best and perhaps only solution of this mysterious word is to examine its meaning. It is a Greek compound. *Nikao* means to have the upper hand, to domineer; *laos* means, the people (our English "laity"). Nicolaitanes signifies "the domineerers of the people." A priestly class had sprung up in the church, domineering over the rest of the people, the so-called laity. And this domineering class claimed a superior place in the body of Christ and a priesthood which rightly belongs to the Lord Jesus Christ. This evil was rejected in Ephesus, but is fully sanctioned and tolerated in Pergamos. Priestly assumption became then, and ever since has been, the corruption of Christianity. This is what our Lord hates and what He hates we must hate with Him.

4. Thyatira, the Period of the Romish Corruption. Verses 18-29. The corruption which set in like a great flood with the fourth century increased till the depths of Satan (verse 24) were reached. Thyatira brings us into the period of the Papacy and its wickedness, ecclesiastical and otherwise. Here our Lord reveals Himself as "the Son of God." Rome speaks more of Him as the son of the virgin, the son of Mary, than as the Son of God. The Roman Catholic apostasy has put a woman in the place of the Son of God. Her corruption is fully revealed in verse 20. Jezebel, who called herself a prophetess, was permitted to teach and seduce God's servants to commit fornication and to eat things sacrificed unto idols. Jezebel the wicked woman represents the Papacy. Jezebel was a heathenish woman married to an Israelitish King. She was a queen and an idolatress and persecuted the true prophets of God (1 Kings xviii-xxi). Apply all this to the Romish church with her spiritual fornication and idolatry. The church—more strictly speaking the Papacy—assumes the place of teacher and dictator; and Christ is rejected. Jezebel has a double meaning. It means "the chaste one" but also means "a dunghill." Rome claims to be the Bride of Christ, but in reality is a dunghill of all vileness and corruption. In verse 21 is another significant statement "she repents not" (repented is incorrect). Rome does not change. She is the same to-day as she was 500 years ago. She exists to-day and will continue in her impenitent state till the predicted doom will overtake her (verse 22; chapter xvii-xviii). In the fourth kingdom parable (Matthew xiii) corresponding to this fourth church-period, our Lord speaks of a woman, who took leaven (corruption) and put it into the fine, pure, three measures of meal (symbolical of the doctrine of Christ). The woman in the parable of the leaven is Rome, the Jezebel in the message to Thyatira.

Chapter III

5. *Sardis, the Period of the Reformation and Protestantism. Verses 1-6.* We have traced briefly the decline during the 1450-1500 years of Church history. The climax is reached in Thyatira, prophetically the Roman abomination and apostasy. In Sardis we see the progress of evil stayed. Roman Catholicism, as already mentioned, is a fixed and unchanging religious system. Rome will yet have for a brief season a startling revival and get back her place as the mistress of the nations. But in Sardis we see a reaction. Sardis means "those escaping." It is the

reformation period, the movement which produced Protestantism. The reformation itself was of God and the great men who were used were the most mighty instruments of the Holy Spirit. It was the greatest work, up to that time, since the days of the apostles. But out of it came the human systems which go by the name of Protestantism. The reformation began well, but soon developed in the different Protestant systems into a dead, lifeless thing. They have a name to live but are dead. This is the verdict of our Lord upon the churches which sprung out of the reformation: "Thou hast a name that thou livest and art dead."

6. *Philadelphia, the Faithful Remnant. Verses 7-13.* Philadelphia means "brotherly love." As Sardis came out of Thyatira, a protest against it, so Philadelphia comes out of Sardis and is a protest against the dead, lifeless, Spiritless condition prevailing in Protestantism. Out of the deadness of the state churches over and over again came forth companies of believers, energized by the Holy Spirit. Philadelphia has been variously applied to Methodism, the evangelical movements, missionary efforts and to the revivals of the nineteenth century. But it is more than that. It is a complete return to the first principles. The message makes this clear. It is the one message (besides Smyrna) in which the Lord does not say "I have against thee," it is that which pleases Him and which He commends. It is a revival and turning back to the first love. The Lord Jesus Christ is once more as the all absorbing object before the heart; Philadelphia repudiates all that dishonors Him and owns alone

that worthy, ineffable Name. It is a faithful remnant
gathering around His Name as there was a faithful
remnant in the closing days of the Old Testament
(Mal. iii: 16-17). All human pretensions are rejected.
The truth of the unity of all believers is owned and
manifested in brotherly love towards all the Saints.
They walk in the path of separation, in self-judgment,
in lowliness of mind; they have a little strength, which
means weakness; they are a feeble few. Twice the
Lord speaks of obedience to His Word. "Thou hast
kept my Word"—"Thou has kept the Word of my
patience." And the Philadelphian does not deny His
Name. These are the two chief characteristics of this
phase of Christianity during the closing days of the
professing Church on earth: Obedience to His Word
and faithfulness and devotion to His Name. The
Word and the Name are denied in the last days. The
apostasy of Christendom consists in the rejection of
the written Word and the living Word. And turning
their backs upon a dead profession, going on in con-
fessed weakness are such paralyzed in their service?
Far from it! The Lord promises to open the door
for service which no man can shut. Every child of
God may test this. True and continued service is the
result of true and continued faithfulness to the Lord.
Especially is this service to be blessed to those who
hold to a perverted Judaism (verse 9). And there is
the great promise for them, which they believe and
hope for, the coming of Himself to keep them out of
the great tribulation (verse 10). In Philadelphia there
is a revival of prophetic truth, an earnest waiting
for the coming of the Lord. Philadelphia is not a

defined church-period, but rather a description of a
loyal remnant called out by the Spirit of God and
bearing the final testimony to the whole counsel of
God by word and deed. If the reader desires to please
the Lord then study the details of the message to
Philadelphia and walk accordingly.

*7. Laodicea, the Indifferent and Apostate Church.
Verses 14-22.* Laodicea means "The judging or rights
of the People." It is opposite of Nicolaitanism. The
domineerers of the people still go on in Rome, but
in Protestantism the people (the laity) arise and claim
their rights and do the judging. This condition was
also foreseen by the Apostle Paul. "For the time will
come when they (the laity) will not endure sound doctrine; but after their own lusts shall they heap to
themselves teachers, having itching ears" (2 Tim.
iv: 3). We see in Laodicea the final religious and
apostate conditions of protestant Christendom and
the complete rejection of the professing body. "I
will spue thee out of my mouth." He Himself is seen
standing outside, which shows that He is rejected.
But infinite Grace! He knocks and is still willing to
come in and bestow the riches of His Grace. And the
Philadelphian-Christian, who is separated from the
Laodicean state, whose heart is filled with the Love
of Christ can learn a lesson here. If our Lord stands
outside and yet knocks and waits in patience, we too
with Him outside of the camp where He is disowned,
can try to gain admittance to Laodicean hearts.
Epaphras did this (Col. iv: 12-13). Laodicea consists in a proudly boasting spirit with total indifference
to the Lord Jesus Christ and to His Name. It is

religiousness without any truth nor the power of the Holy Spirit. Lukewarmness expresses it all. "Lukewarmness, a perfect jumble of sacred and wordly matters. The word does not point chiefly to half-heartedness. But as lukewarmness is produced by pouring of hot and cold water together into the same vessel, so in the Laodicean state, intense wordliness will be varnished over by plausible and humanitarian and religious pretences." Great reformation movements for the advancement of religion and the betterment of the world, the rejection of the Gospel as the power of God unto salvation, are characteristic features of this final phase of Christendom. It will continue and wax worse and worse till His patience is exhausted. Then the true church will be caught up with the departed Saints to meet Him in the air, and Laodicea will be spued out of His mouth. It is important to notice that Thyatira (Rome), Sardis (Protestantism) and the two phases of Protestantism represented by Philadelphia and Laodicea co-exist. They go on together. This is seen by the fact that in each our Lord speaks of His second coming (ii: 25; iii: 3; iv: 10-11, 16). The Lord takes His own to Himself. Rome and an apostate Protestant Christendom continue on earth during the period of judgment, preceding the visible coming of the Lord.

III. The Things Which Are After These. The End of the Age. The Consummation and the Final Messages

Chapters IV-XXII

FIRST SUBDIVISION. THE HEAVENLY SCENE. BEFORE THE THRONE.

Chapters IV-V

Chapter IV. *The Open Door and the Vision of the Throne. Verses 1-3.* The scene changes suddenly. We are no longer on earth but are transported into heaven. The true church is gone and the apostate Church while still on earth to pass into the judgments of the great tribulation, is no longer owned by the Lord and therefore not mentioned. That is why the word "church" disappears entirely from this book after the third chapter. The open door and the voice which calls "come up hither" and John's presence in glory in the spirit, clearly indicate symbolically the fulfilment of 1 Thess. iv: 15-17. That for which the faithful remnant waited, the blessed hope of the Church, has suddenly come to pass. The departure of the true Church from the earth will be as sudden as its beginning (Acts ii: 1-2). Surely the gathering of all the Saints in glory must some day take place. He promised it (John xiv: 1-3). He prayed for it (John xvii: 24). The Holy Spirit in the Epistles bears constant witness to it. The shout, perhaps the same words which John heard "Come up hither," will open the graves of all the Saints, and those who are on earth at that time will be caught up; yes dear reader, we are authorized to say "we who remain shall be caught up together with them in clouds to meet the Lord in the air."

John's first vision in heaven is the established throne, the sign and symbol of the universal government of God. While thrones on earth begin to totter and to fall and man's day closes in the predicted upheavals, there is a throne which cannot be affected nor disturbed. Yea, He who sitteth there and looks down upon earth and sees man's rebellion and madness laughs at them and holds them in derision (Psalm ii: 4). The occupant of the throne was to look upon like a Jasper and a Sardine stone. They were the first and the last precious stones in the breastplate of the High priest, only the Sardine stone is there the first while here it is mentioned last. The names of Benjamin ("the son of the right hand") and Reuben (behold a son!) were engraven upon these two stones (Exod. xviii: 17-20). The Sardine, probably identical with the ruby, is a blood-red stone. The Jasper is not the common Jasper of little value. See chapter xxi: 11. Many think it is the diamond or perhaps the opal. Our Lord and the glory of His Person are thus symbolically represented in these stones. His glory in the brilliant stone, His redemption work in the blood-red Sardine. The rainbow in emerald-green tells us that in the judgments about to come upon the earth mercy will be also remembered. It is the covenant sign. Though judgments come, yet mercy is in store for Israel and the earth.

2. *The Twenty-four Elders. Verse 4.* Who is

represented by these twenty-four elders? They cannot be angels. Angels are never seen seated upon thrones, (not seats as in the authorized version) nor are they crowned, nor can they sing redemption's song as the Elders do. There is only one possible meaning. They represent the redeemed, the Saints in glory. They are Priests (clothed in white) and they are Kings (crowned); they are the royal priesthood in the presence of the throne. And why twenty-four? It points us back to the work David did for the temple. He appointed twenty-four courses of the priests (1 Chron. xxiv). Twice twelve would suggest the Saints of the Old and New Testament.

3. *The Description of the Throne. Verse 5.* There were lightnings and voices and thunderings. This is repeatedly stated. See viii: 5; xi: 18; xvi: 18. It is the symbol of God's throne in its judicial aspect. And He who occupies that throne is our Lord. Heaven's throne, so to speak, is getting ready for the judgments. And the Elders are in perfect peace, undisturbed by these otherwise terrifying manifestations, sitting before the throne. There is no judgment for them, they are safe at home.

4. *The Four Living Creatures and the Great Praise and Worship. Verses 6-11.* The sea of glass is a reminder of the great laver in Solomon's temple in which the priests had to wash. Now it is solidified because no more water is needed for the cleansing of the Saints. The word "beast" should be changed to "living creatures" or "living ones." They are not symbolical of the church, or a special class of saints, but they are the same supernatural beings seen in the

Old Testament and always in connection with the throne and the presence of Jehovah. They are the cherubim of Ezekiel's great vision, chapters i and x. Their constant cry, "Holy, Holy," reminds us of the seraphim also. (Isaiah vi). The worship here is the worship of Him who is the Creator.

"The saints here fall down before the throne, bow themselves before His place in glory, and worship Him in His endless being, and lay down their given glory before His supreme and proper glory, ascribing all glory to Him, as alone worthy of it; but here, according to the nature of the celebration of it, the Creator for whom all things are. In all changes these remained true. It will be remarked here, that the living creatures only celebrate and declare; the Elders worship with understanding. All through the Revelation the Elders give their reason for worshipping. There is spiritual intelligence in them." *

Chapter V. *1. Who is worthy to Open the Book? Verses 1-3.* Much has been written about the meaning of the book written within and sealed with seven seals. What the book contains is no secret whatever. Beginning with the sixth chapter the seals are opened and after they are all broken the contents of the book are made known. The book contains the judgments for this earth preceding His coming in power and glory and the beginning of His reign. It is therefore the book of the righteous judgments of God, preceding the glorious manifestation of the King of kings. The same figure of a book is found in Ezekiel

---

* Synopsis.

ii: 9-10. And who is worthy to open this book and make known, as well as execute, its contents?

2. The Answer. Verses 4-5. John receives the answer to the question the strong angel had proclaimed. One of the Elders told him "Behold the lion of the tribe of Judah, the Root of David, has prevailed to open the book, and the seven seals thereof." No further comment is needed; the Lord Jesus Christ is the Lion of Judah and the Root of David. "The King's wrath is as a roaring lion" (Prov. xix: 12). He is now to be revealed in mighty power and strength to execute Judgment. See Genesis xlix: 9. And He is also the Root of David. Both terms tell us that Judah and the house of David will be remembered in mercy when the judgment sweeps over the earth. The time is at hand when the Davidic covenant-promise will be fully accomplished by Him who is the Lion of the tribe of Judah.

3. The Vision of the Lamb. Verses 6-7. And now He is seen who alone is worthy to open the book. He does not appear as a Lion in majesty, but He is seen by John as a Lamb standing, as having been·slain. The Lamb slain is the Lion. His victory was gained by dying, and therefore He must have as the Lion the victory over all His enemies. Thrice the number seven is repeated revealing His perfection. Notice especially three descriptions. He is "in the midst." He is the center of God's government and of heaven itself, as He is for His people the center of all their thoughts and affections. He is seen "as a Lamb standing." Now He is seated at the right hand of God, but when the time comes when His enemies are about

to be made His footstool, He will arise to act. He
will arise and have mercy upon Zion (Psalm cii: 12).
And He is seen as "the Lamb slain." The Greek word
here suggests "slain in sacrifice." In His body after
His resurrection the disciples saw the nail-prints and
the wound the spear had made (John xx: 20, 25, 27).
Here when He is about to take to Himself His rights,
purchased by His death on the cross, about to usher
in His reign, the wound-prints are also seen. And
when He comes in great power and glory the same
tokens of His passion will be visible, for they shall
look on Him whom they pierced. And what an indescribable scene when He took the book!

*4. The Worship of the Living Creatures and the
Elders. Verses 8-10.* A great worship scene follows
at once. The four living Creatures join in with the
Elders, but the latter alone have harps and golden
bowls full of incense, which are the prayers of the
Saints. The harps express their great joy and praise
and the bowls full of incense denote the priestly
ministry of the redeemed. Such is part of our glorious
future, an endless praise of deepest joy, and perfect
ministry. The prayers of the Saints are not the
prayers of the past, but the prayers of Jewish saints,
so beautifully re-written in the Psalms, when the
time of Jacob's trouble is on the earth. And then
the new song! This is redemption's song, the song
of redeeming love; the old song was the praise of God
as the Creator in His glory (Job xxxviii: 7). Redemption is now accomplished for the Saints in glory;
they look forward to the glorious manifestation with
Himself and the great new song bursts forth in all

its wonderful meaning. Better rendering is "Worthy art Thou to take the book, and to open the seals thereof; for Thou wast slain, and didst purchase unto God by Thy blood, out of every tribe, and tongue, and people, and nation and madest them unto our God kings and priests, and they shall reign over the earth." He and His worthiness are the great theme. He is worthy; He was slain; He hath purchased; He purchased the glory for His own. No other worship will be known in heaven. Happy are we if we sing redemption's song down here in blessed anticipation of the soon coming consummation, when we shall see Him as He is "in the midst" and enter upon our never ending and glorious inheritance.

5. *The Worthiness of the Lamb Acclaimed by all Beings. Verses 11-14.* Praise of Him becomes universe-wide. The innumerable company of angels join in it. "The number of them was myriads of myraids and thousands of thousands." * And the Praise described here leads us on to the time when God will be all in all. It is the never ending praise, the Hallelujah-chorus of redeemed Creation! The four living creatures say "Amen"; the Elders worship. Omit "Him that liveth forever and ever," as these words do not belong here.

---

* This is according to the Greek.

SECOND DIVISION. THE OPENING OF THE SEVEN SEALS.

Chapters VI-VIII: 5

The Lamb, invested with all the authority to execute judgment, having received His commission from God, begins now to open the seals of the book which is in His hands, the hands which were once nailed to the cross. It is evident that the breaking of the seals does not begin till His Saints are gathered around the throne in glory. Until then it is still the day of grace. Read Isaiah lxi: 1-2 and compare with Luke iv: 18-19. When He read from the book in the synagogue of Nazareth, He stopped with the sentence "to proclaim the acceptable year of the Lord." He did not read "and the day of vengeance of our God." When the Saints are gathered home, when the true Church is received into glory, the acceptable year of the Lord ends. The door will be shut as far as the nations of Christendom are concerned and the days of vengeance will be executed.*

In Matthew xxiv, in the great prophetic Olivet Discourse, our Lord speaks of the end of the age. It is the end of the interrupted Jewish age, the final seven years of the prophecy in Daniel (Chapter ix). The first thing which our Lord mentions is, what He calls, "the beginning of sorrows" (Matt. xxiv: 8). This is fulfilled in the seal judgments.

Chapter VI. *1. The First Seal. The White Horse: the Conquering Rider. Verses 1-2.* When the first seal is opened one of the living creatures said in voice

---

* But see Chap. VII.

of thunder: "Come." The words "and see" must be
omitted here and in verses 3, 5 and 7. A rider upon
a white horse appears; his is a bloodless conquest.
He has a bow, but no arrow. He receives a crown and
goes forth to conquer. Many expositors make this
rider the Lord Jesus or some power which represents
Him. It is positively incorrect. The Lord is indeed
pictured as a rider upon a white horse, but when He
comes it will be at the close of the judgment and
tribulation period and His victorious conquest will be
far different from the rider under the first seal.
Read carefully Psalm xlv: 1-5; Zech. ix: 9-14; Rev.
xix: 11, etc., also the Apocalypse of Zechariah, especially chapters i-ii. The rider here is a great counterfeit leader, not the personal Anti-christ, but the little
horn which Daniel saw coming out of the ten-horned
beast (Daniel vii). We are now in the most solemn
and ominous times the world has ever known. Many
are the voices which are calling for a European confederacy and for some great leader, another Napoleon.
The blinded world looks for such a one and expects
that he will bring peace and order into the prevailing
chaos. And the Lord will permit such a one to come,
deceiving the world so that they will say "peace and
safety" (1 Thess. v: 1-3). This coming leader of the
revived Roman empire will go forth to conquer and
become its political head. He is Satan's man as we
shall see later. No human being knows how long God,
in His infinite patience, may still delay the beginning
of all these things. But as far as mortal eye can
see, enlightened by His Word and Spirit, these things
are at hand and the outcome of the European war

may be this confederacy and the rider upon the white horse will begin his conquest. And if so, how near, how very near, the home-gathering of the Saints must be. And this is the first thing our Lord mentions in the Olivet Discourse, to take place as the age ends: false Christs, deceivers (Matt. xxiv: 4-5).

2. The Second Seal. The Red Horse. The Rider With the Great Sword. Verses 3-4. The second seal reveals a rider upon a red horse. He takes away the false peace, which the rider upon the white horse as a divine judgment act established. The universal peace of which the world dreams without the presence of the Prince of Peace, will be of a short duration. Another awful war follows. It will not be war alone between nation and nation, but it will be a world-wide reign of terror and bloodshed, a carnage unknown before in the history of the world. Not a few believe that the present war is the second seal. But this cannot be because the true Church is still here. Something far worse is in store for the earth. Even keen observers in the world say that this will not be the last war the world will see. Blessed be His Name! that we His people will escape these coming judgments. See in Matthew xxiv how our Lord mentions the great conflict of nation against nation and kingdom against kingdom.

3. The Third Seal. The Black Horse. The Rider With the Balance. Verses 5-6. The black horse rider brings famine. Exactly what our Lord mentions next: "there shall be famines." Famine follows war and inasmuch as the second seal brings the greatest war, the third seal will bring the greatest famine. The judgments of God are then on the earth. It has been estimated that a denarius (wrongly translated penny) was about one dollar and a half in our money, and a measure of wheat, a "choenix" about one of our quarts. A quart of wheat for a dollar and a half. Starvation will come then for countless thousands. The rich seem to escape a part of this judgment for the oil and the wine, the luxuries of the well to do, are not to be hurt. They will receive their share of judgment later. Our Lord also speaks of famines in Matthew xxiv.

4. *The Fourth Seal. The Pale Horse. The Rider Followed by Hades. Verses 7-8.* The next rider under the fourth seal is named death. And Hades, the region of the unseen, (not hell) is populated. Sword, hunger, death, that is pestilences and the beasts of the earth, claim an awful harvest (Ezek. xiv: 21). And so our Lord spoke of "pestilences." These four seal judgments are hardening judgments. The Christless masses of Christendom will not recognize the hand of God in these awful visitations. It is different in the present war of Europe because the testimony of the Gospel is still given, backed by the prayers of God's people. But after the true Church is gone and the Lord has spued out Laodicea these judgments will only harden their hearts.

5. *The Fifth Seal. The Cry of the Souls Under the Altar. Verses 9-11.* The four living Creatures have uttered their fourfold "Come." They are thus seen in connection with the providential government of the world. Under the fifth seal the scene changes completely. John saw under the altar the souls of them that had been slain. And they cry, "How long,

O Lord!" Who are they? Not the martyrs of past ages. They are risen from the dead and are in glory with redeemed bodies. The words of the Lord in the Olivet Discourse give us the key. Speaking to His Jewish disciples He said: "Then shall they deliver you up, and shall kill you and ye shall be hated of all nations for my Name's sake" (Matt. xxiv:9). The Lord speaks of another company of Jewish disciples who will bear a witness during the end of the age, after the rapture of the Church. He will not leave Himself without a witness. He calls a remnant of His people Israel and they bear a witness to the coming of the Messiah, their coming deliverer and King. Many of them suffer martyrdom. Their cry, "How long?" is the well known prayer of Jewish saints; and their prayer to have their blood avenged is equally a Jewish prayer. Christians are not supplicating for vengeance on their foes. The prayer for vengeance refers us to the imprecatory psalms prewritten by the Holy Spirit in anticipation of the final persecution of Jewish believers. And the fellow servants and their brethren who are yet to be killed (verse 11) are the martyrs of that remnant during the final three and one-half years, which is the great tribulation. See them mentioned in chapter xx:4. Notice the classes there. But there is only one class under the fifth seal, those slain in the first half of the week, before the image of the beast was set up. The Saints whom Daniel mentions (Dan. vii:27) who receive the Kingdom are these Jewish Saints. The Saints of the Most High as mentioned by Daniel are not the church-saints.

6. *The Sixth Seal. The Shaking of all Things. The*

Anticipation of the End. Verses 12-17. Are the things mentioned under this seal to be taken in a literal sense or symbolically? Most of it is symbolical, yet at the same time great physical phenomena are also involved. The earthquake possibly means a literal earthquake. "Earthquakes in diverse places" our Lord predicted. And they increase as the age draws to its close. But the language is symbolical. Everything is being shaken in this poor world. The civil and governmental powers on earth all go to pieces; every class from kings to slaves is affected by it and terrorized. The political and ecclesiastical world is going to pieces. See the list of symbolical names and their meaning at the close of this volume. And when these shaking times have come, when thrones fall and anarchy reigns, when the great collapse of civilization and human society has come with signs on earth and in heaven, the earth-dwellers will see in anticipation the approaching day of wrath. Terror fills every breast and those who sneered at prayer, as the Christ-rejectors do now, will gather for a prayer-meeting to appeal to the rocks to cover them. Read the following Old Testament passages in connection with this seal. Isaiah xxiv; xxxiv: 2-4; Joel ii: 30-31; Zephaniah i; Haggai ii: 6-7.

BETWEEN THE SIXTH AND SEVENTH SEAL. A PARENTHETICAL VISION.

Chapter VII

Chapter VII. *1. The Remnant of Israel Called and Sealed. Verses 1-8.* We reach now the first paren-

thetical vision. It must not be taken chronologically.
The six seal judgments extend over the entire period
of the age ending. The rider upon the white horse
will be on the scene to the end; wars will continue to
the end, and culminate in the battle of Armageddon,
and so do the famines and pestilences. And the sixth
seal brings the end in view. We shall see the correspondence with the seventh trumpet and seventh vial
later. The trumpet and vial judgments are more
intense and more terrible than the seal judgments.
In a certain sense they are parallel; the effect of each
is continuously felt. The parenthetical vision of the
seventh chapter also covers the entire period of the
last seven years and brings before us even the vision
of what will be after the great tribulation.

How much confusion would have been avoided if
expositors and Christians in searching for the meaning
of this vision, had not lost sight of two great facts
1. This chapter can have no application to the Church
on earth, nor to the Church in glory, for the simple
reason that the Church is already complete and translated to glory. 2. The vision states clearly that the
sealed company is "of all the tribes of the children of
Israel." There are to-day perhaps a score or more of
little sects who all claim to be the 144,000. Holiness
sects, Advent sects, healers, Pentecostal people and
others, all claim to be *the* company. If the true interpretation of Revelation is seen, that this company is
called after the rapture of the Church, these confusing
theories will at once be rejected.

The sealed company is of Israel. After the Church
is removed to glory, when the fulness of the Gentiles

is come in (Rom. xi: 26) the Lord will turn in mercy
to Israel and call, before the judgments fall, a remnant
which will also be sealed (See Ezek. ix). This remnant is frequently seen on the pages of Old Testament
prophecy. We read prophetically their longings and
their prayers. We quote a few passages of the many:
Ps. xliv: 10-26; lv-lvii; lxiv; lxxix; lxxx; Isaiah lxiii:
15-lxiv. This remnant, enlightened by the Holy Spirit,
will pass through the entire seven years. Many of
them will suffer martyrdom, but the greater part will
pass through the entire tribulation, enduring to the
end, and then saved by their King, our Lord, when
He comes in glory. The so-called orthodox Jews
will probably constitute with members of the other
tribes* this remnant. The number, 144,000, that is,
12,000 out of each tribe, must be looked upon as symbolical. It speaks of the complete government, which
as to the earth, is invested in a redeemed and restored
Israel. Dan is not mentioned because that tribe seems
to be identified with Satan's work during the tribulation (See Gen. xlix: 17). It is said the anti-Christ will
be of the tribe of Dan. This sealed company also
bears a great testimony. They are the preachers of
the Gospel of the Kingdom, as a witness to all nations
before the end comes (Matt. xxiv: 14). Therefore
during the time when the judgments are executed from
above there will be a world-wide preaching of the
Gospel of the Kingdom, proclaiming the coming of the
King, calling to repentance and faith in His Name, and
offering mercy still.

---

* No one knows where the ten tribes are; but God knows
and He will bring them to light at that time.

2. The Saved Multitude of Gentiles Coming Out of the Great Tribulation. Verses 9-17. The application of this passage of Scripture to the redeemed Church in glory is wrong. This Scripture does not apply to the Church in glory, but to saved Gentiles on earth. It is a company which comes "out of the great tribulation." The Church enters the glory before that great tribulation begins. The great multitude represents those Gentiles who will hear the final testimony and believe. They will have turned in repentance to Him and will be washed in His precious Blood. Our Lord speaks of them in the great judgment of the nations as sheep, who stand at His right hand and inherit the Kingdom (Matt. xxv: 31, etc.). The brethren of our Lord mentioned in Matthew are the remnant of Israel. For a complete exposition see "The Gospel of Matthew," by the author of this volume. This great company therefore does not stand before a heavenly throne, but before the millennial throne on earth. It is a millennial scene after the tribulation is passed. Sometimes the question is asked: Will there be another chance for the Gospel hardened multitudes of Laodicean Christendom during the tribulation? Will the large number of nominal Christians accept the final message given through the remnant of Israel? In view of 2 Thess. ii: 1-12 we are bound to answer this question negatively. This great company is gathered from *all* nations, many of whom never heard a message of mercy before. The temple mentioned is the millennial temple (Ezek. xl-xliv). And then there is a description of the millennial blessings for these redeemed nations.

Chapter VIII. *The Seventh Seal. Verses 1-5.*
The silence in heaven when the seventh seal is opened
is indicative of the solemn things which are now to
come. The scroll is now fully opened and there
is an ominous hush as the seven angels prepare to
sound their trumpets of judgment. John beholds these
seven angels, but before they begin to sound
"another angel" is seen standing at the altar.
This angel is not a creature, but like *the* angel
of Jehovah in the Old Testament, is our Lord
Himself. He is seen as the Priest in behalf
of the praying, suffering Saints on earth. No
angel can offer the prayers of the Saints, but He,
who is the one Intercessor alone can do that. And
for what do they pray on earth? For mercy for those
who persecute the remnant of Israel? No! They
pray for divine intervention, for the fire of judgment
as Elijah did. And therefore the Lord answers them
accordingly. He fills the censer with fire off the altar
of God's holiness and casts it into the earth. And
there were voices, and thunderings, and lightnings,
and an earthquake.

**THIRD DIVISION. THE SOUNDING OF THE
SEVEN TRUMPETS.**
Chapters VIII: 6-XI: 18.

Chapter VIII. *1. The First Trumpet. Verses 6-7.*
The judgments which follow can hardly be fully interpreted at this time. It would be folly to dogmatize
about them. The historical application we reject, because the scope of the book makes it clear that these
judgments have not yet taken place. What many of

these things mean may perhaps never be fully understood till they are actually in fulfillment. The first four trumpet judgments evidently stand by themselves. The cry for judgment from the suffering and persecuted remnant of God's ancient people is answered in what happens on the earth. The fire the Lord cast down is doing its work. The first trumpet manifests the same evidences of divine wrath as came upon Egypt, when Israel suffered there, under the seventh plague (Exodus ix:23). Hail (heat withdrawn), fire and blood are all the symbols of divine wrath. The trees and the green grass were burned up. The green things are symbols of agricultural and commercial prosperity. All is then passing and man's boasted prosperity ends in great calamity. The third part mentioned repeatedly in these trumpet judgments refers to the Roman empire. Terrible devastation by different agencies, including burning heat,* will sweep over that empire.

2. The Second Trumpet. Verses 8-9. That this is not a literal mountain is obvious. A mountain in Scripture language represents a Kingdom (Isaiah ii: 2; Zech. iv:7; Psalm xlvi:2; and especially Jerem. li:25). The sea is typical of nations. Some kingdom, internally on fire, signifying probably revolution, will be precipitated into the restless sea of nations, and the result will be a still greater destruction of life and commerce, which is represented by the ships.

3. The Third Trumpet. Verses 10-11. In the preceding trumpets things were cast upon the earth, but

---

* Burning heat may be symbolical of intolerant despotism.

here is a star which falls. It is some person who claimed authority and who becomes an apostate, whose fall produces the awful results given here. It may be the final anti-Christ who first may have claimed to be for Israel a great teacher with divine authority and then takes the awful plunge. Worm-wood is his name and the waters became worm-wood and bitter. It stands for great corruption.

4. The Fourth Trumpet. Verses 12-13. The sun, the moon and the stars are now affected. The sun is the symbol of the highest authority, the moon, who has not her own light, is symbolical of derived authority and the stars are symbolical of subordinate authority. The symbolical meaning of this trumpet judgment is that all authority within the revived Roman empire will be smitten by the hand from above and as a result there will be the most awful moral darkness. These four trumpet judgments tell of prosperity taken first from the earth; a great power burning with the fires of revolution affecting the nations; a great leader will fall and become worm-wood; and authority disowned and smitten will fill the territory of the Roman empire with the densest darkness. Before this great war we have often heard it said how impossible all this sounds. No one can say so any longer. Europe's condition is appalling and what will it be when these judgments fall!

Chapter IX. *5. The Fifth Trumpet. Verses 1-12.* The remaining three trumpets have a "woe" attached to each. This is announced in the last verse of the preceding chapter where the word angel should be "eagle." An eagle, the bird of prey, proclaims the three-fold woe. He acts thus as a herald of **great** judgments (Matt. xxiv: 28, Rev. xix: 17-18). **The** fifth trumpet is a special judgment upon apostate Israel; because those who suffer are they "which have not the seal of God on their foreheads" (verse 4). The great tribulation in the second half of the week, comes now into prominence. If we turn to chapter xii: 12 we read something similar to the eagle's message of woe. "Woe unto the inhabiters of the earth and of the sea! for the devil is come down unto you, having great wrath, because he knoweth that he hath but a short time." Preceding the sounding of the fifth trumpet the eagle proclaimed the woe upon the inhabiters of the earth. The star which is seen fallen from heaven with the key of the pit of the abyss is Satan himself cast out of heaven. The details of this event we learn in the twelfth chapter. He has the key to the pit of the abyss, the same word "deep," used in Luke viii: 31. "And they (the demons) besought Him that He would not command them to go out into the deep (abyss)." He unlocks the prison house of the fallen angels and the most awful satanic agencies come forth to begin their awful work of torment. The smoke first, symbolical of darkening; the locusts next, symbolical of these demon powers. Awful darkness prevails and the most diabolical delusions, producing fearful torments among apostate Israel and the inhabiters of the earth. It is the time of the strong delusion (2 Thess. ii: 4-11) which has come. And over them is a King. His name is given in Greek and Hebrew, showing that it is both Jew and Gentile that come under His power. Both names mean the same—"destruction." Apostate Israel and also apostate Christendom will suffer greatly under this trumpet judgment and face the desolation of everything religious.   The light is now completely blotted out and in the darkness coming from the pit of the abyss the demon powers will do their fearful work.   Demonpossession and the most awful torments for soul and body will be the general thing.   Because this judgment also concerns apostate Christendom the Greek name of the destroyer is given besides the Hebrew.

2. The Sixth Trumpet. The Second Woe. Verses 13-21.   The sixth angel is commanded by a voice from the horns of the golden altar to loose the four angels who are bound at Euphrates, and as a result an innumerable company of horsemen is released.*   They are prepared for a specific time to do their work.   Euphrates is once more mentioned under the pouring out of the sixth vial.   We believe the sixth vial judgment gives the key to these horsemen here.   Euphrates does not mean the Turkish empire as we shall more fully show when we come to the sixth vial.   This river was both the boundary line of the old Roman empire and the land of Israel.   Restraining influences held back the tide of nations on the other side of the river; this restraint is now removed and therefore a great invasion takes place.   As the land of Israel is nearest it will suffer first, but the revived Roman empire will be the objective of these invading hordes.   The "third part" stands for the Roman empire, the

---

* Greek: twice ten thousand times ten thousand, that is 200 million.   The number would indicate the immense, uncountable hordes.

coming European confederacy. This invasion is under the King of the North. It is seen in its beginning here and is consummated under the sixth vial. There the "Kings of the Sunrise" are included. And under the sixth vial they are more specifically gathered for the great day of God Almighty. We refer the reader to chapter xvi: 12. The four angels have been variously interpreted. They must not be identified with the angels in chapter vii: 1. We can only say again that these things will be fully known when they are taking place. Connected with this invasion there is another manifestation of demon power. Serpents are mentioned. The Serpent, Satan, and his serpents, demons, are then on the earth. Everything is under Satanic control. The great mass of Apostates who escaped these plagues did not repent. They have become so blinded that they worship idols again, and demons, and connected with it are the grossest immoralities.

BETWEEN THE SIXTH AND SEVENTH TRUMPET PARENTHETICAL VISIONS.

Chapters X-XI: 14.

As there is a parenthesis between the breaking of the sixth and seventh seals so is there between the sixth and seventh trumpet and another between the sixth and seventh vial.

Chapter X. *1. The Descending Angel. Verses 1-7.* The proclamation of the mighty angel is the first recorded event in this parenthesis. Who is this angel?

It is Christ Himself. We saw our Lord in angel's form before the opening of the seventh seal and then He appeared in *priestly* dignity. Here before the sounding of the seventh trumpet he appears again in the same form, but He is called a mighty angel and we behold Him in *royal* dignity. The cloud, the rainbow, the face like the sun, His right foot upon the sea, the left on the earth, the voice like a lion and the seven thunders, all declare this to be correct. The hour is rapidly approaching when the kingdoms of this earth are to become His Kingdom. This is seen under the seventh trumpet. And therefore He is seen now in this attitude of royal dignity. The words which He speaks (verses 6 and 7) bear out this interpretation. "There shall be time no longer" means "there shall be no longer delay." Man's day is about to close. The mystery of God is now to be finished "as He hath declared to His servants, the prophets," or in better rendering "the mystery of God also shall be completed according to the good tidings which He declared by His own servants, the prophets." How great has been that mystery! Evil had apparently triumphed; the heavens for so long have been silent. Satan had been permitted to be the god of this age deceiving the nations. And Israel, too, is included in this mystery. And now the time has come when the mystery of God will be completed, when the glorious messages, the good tidings of the prophets concerning Israel's blessing and the kingdom will be fulfilled.

2. *The Little Book. Verses 8-11.* But what is the little book which the angel holds in His right hand?

It is not a sealed book, but open. It stands for the prophecies in the Old Testament relating especially to Israel during the time of the great tribulation, what is yet to come upon the earth, culminating in the personal and glorious appearing of the Lord to begin His millennial reign. But we do not need to say more. We saw the contents of the seven-sealed book in chapter five were made known when the Lamb opened the seals. And the contents of the little book we shall also know. What follows after the parenthesis takes us upon Jewish ground and shows the fulfillment of these prophecies. And John was commanded to eat the book (See Ezek. ii: 8-iii: 3). It was sweet and bitter. Such is the prophetic Word concerning these things. Sweet because it tells of deliverance and a glorious consummation, but when it is digested, taken in, it reveals the bitterness, the sorrows and judgments which are connected with it. And John had more to prophesy in connection with the end, concerning peoples, nations, tongues and many kings. And this we find in the chapters which follow.

Chapter XI. *3. The Temple, Altar and Jewish Worshippers. Verses 1-2.* We see at once how Jewish things come now into view. To apply these verses to the Church and make the temple the Church is absolutely wrong. The temple and the altar are Jewish; the holy city is Jerusalem. After the Church has left the earth the Jewish people will be fully restored to their own land, and their land restored to them. They will possess Jerusalem once more. It is even revealed that a power beyond the land of Israel,

friendly to the Jews, will be used in this restoration
(Isaiah xviii). It is deeply significant to read during
this present world-crisis of the soon coming disposi-
tion of Palestine. In the daily press and in magazines
the suggestion is made that Palestine should be handed
over to the Jews. When one follows the history of
Zionism aiming at the establishment of a Jewish State
and now sees how European nations begin to recognize
the claims of the Jews, and promise their help in
their restoration, one cannot but feel that these things
are very near. A partial restoration may be looked
for even now while the true Church is still here.
When the Jews are once more masters in their own
promised land they will erect another temple and
then restore the Levitical worship as far as it is possible. Such a temple must be in Jerusalem (see Isaiah
lxvi: 1-4). In that temple the personal Anti-christ,
the beast out of the land of whom we shall read in
chapter xiii, will appear and claim divine worship.
See 2 Thess. ii: 3-4. Apostate Israel in corrupt alliance with equally apostate Gentiles is seen in the
opening verses of this eleventh chapter, as the court
without the temple. But in the midst of this corrupt
mass, which will follow the delusion of the Anti-christ
and accept Satan's man as their Messiah, there will be
the God-fearing remnant. This remnant is here
divinely recognized as worshippers. Therefore that
coming temple is called "the temple of God" because
the Lord owns the true worshippers found in the midst
of the unbelieving mass. These godly Jews form an
inner circle. The inner place is symbolical of the
faithful remnant of worshippers; the outer court is

the symbol of apostate Israel. The forty-two months are now mentioned for the first time in Revelation. They are identical with the 1,260 days, for forty-two months make this number of days, the times, time and half a time in the prophecy of Daniel, the last three and one-half years of the seventieth week of Daniel.* To make these forty-two months 1,260 years, as it has been done by many expositors, is a mere invention and lacks Scriptural support. These 1,260 days are the time of the great tribulation. Then Israel apostate will be in the worst condition, demon-possessed and idolatrous (Matt. xii: 43-45). Then the Gentiles will do their final devastation of Jerusalem and her worst history will come to pass. She will have to drink the cup of the Lord's fury to the very dregs. We suggest at this point a careful reading of Psalm lxxix and a comparison with this eleventh chapter. It is the prayer of the godly remnant. On the measuring see also Zech. ii.

4. *The Two Witnesses. Verses 3-6.* Much has been written on these two witnesses who will then appear in Jerusalem. The historical school of interpretation has named numerous persons and companies of people, like the Waldenses and Albigenses, who suffered under the papal persecutions. These claims are not in harmony with the divisions of the book, to which we believe it to be our duty to adhere. These two witnesses are still future. Their work will be done during the great tribulation. Others make them

---

* We cannot enlarge upon this interesting prophecy so absolutely necessary for an understanding of this part of Revelation. We refer the reader to Appendix I.

Enoch and Elijah and others think they will be Moses and Elijah returned in person. Some have claimed to be a re-incarnation of Elijah. Such claims are fanatical. No second coming of Moses is anywhere promised in the Word. Something, however, is said about the work of Elijah in the future (Mal. iv: 5-6). But the words of our Lord in Matt. xi: 14, speaking of John the Baptist, and Matt. xvii: 12, seem to make it clear that no literal coming of the same Elijah, who went into glory, without dying, is meant. Yet the deeds of these two witnesses clearly link them with the work of Moses and Elijah. They each do both the things that Moses and Elijah did separately. We take it then that these two witnesses represent the great testimony to be given in Jerusalem during the 1,260 days of the great tribulation. Perhaps the leaders will be two great instruments, manifesting the spirit of Moses and Elijah, endowed with supernatural power, but a large number of witnesses is unquestionably in view here. They maintain in the midst of the Satanic scenes a powerful testimony for God. They are called "olive trees," because the energy and power of the Holy Spirit rest upon them. See and compare with Zech. iv. Their testimony, besides witnessing against the awful corruption, is the Gospel of the Kingdom and the glorious coming of the King. The judgments through them are their credentials.

5. *The Beast and the Witnesses. Verse 7.* In verse 2 the period of the great tribulation was mentioned for the first time and here we have the first mention

of the Beast. This Beast coming out of the pit of the abyss, the deep, is the revived Roman empire under the little horn, seen by Daniel on the four-horned beast (Dan. vii: 8). While he dominates over the Gentiles, he will turn in fury against these Jewish Saints, and the two witnesses will be slain. He makes war with the godly remnant. (Dan. vii: 21). A part of that remnant will be killed. Then the company of martyrs mentioned in vi: 11 will be gathered. This is more fully described in chapter xiii. Here we look at it and the outcome in a general way.

6. *The Treatment of the Slain Witnesses. Verses 8-10.* See again Psalm lxxix: 1-3. The vileness of these coming days of Satan's rule on earth is seen in the treatment of the bodies of Jehovah's servants. The wicked are so elated over the silencing of the testimony that they refuse to permit their burial so that they may feast their eyes upon the sickening spectacle. They rejoice and make it a festive occasion, because torment had come to their consciences through the testimony of the slain. Gentiles, who side with apostate Israel are mentioned, but especially a class which is called "they that dwell on the earth" rejoices over the end of the witnesses. The same class is mentioned several times. Study the passages where they are mentioned: Chapter iii: 10, vi: 9, 10; viii: 13; xi: 9, 10; xiii: 8; xiv: 6, 7; xvii: 8. They are the apostate, nominal Christians who are utterly blinded and hardened. Phil. iii: 18-19 gives their character and destiny. They claim possession of the earth as belonging to them, but God is not only the God of heaven, He is also "the God of the earth." (Rev. xi: 4.)

7. *Their Public Vindication. Verses 11-12.* God's power is manifested in their physical resurrection and their visible translation. Their enemies see a great miracle. The apostates who ridicule even now a physical resurrection, who sneer at the blessed Hope of a coming translation of the Saints, will witness these two great facts. No wonder that a great fear fell upon them. The raised witnesses belong to the first resurrection (xx: 4).

8. *The Great Earthquake. Verses 13-14.* The terror becomes still greater when the whole city is shaken by a mighty earthquake. This is not a symbolical earthquake but a convulsion of nature by which the fourth part of the city falls and 7,000 men are killed. It marks the end of the second woe. Then those who escaped the visitation gave glory unto the God of heaven. It is only inspired by fear. They do not turn in repentance unto God. Here ends the parenthetical vision.

9. *The Seventh Trumpet. The Third Woe. Verses 15-18.* The seventh trumpet brings us to the very end of the tribulation and to the beginning of the millennial reign. It is Jerusalem's deliverance. He who alone is worthy receives the Kingdom. How clear this ought to make the fact that our Lord has no earthly Kingdom now, but He receives the promised Kingdom on the earth at the end of these things. See Dan. vii: 14. Heaven worships too; they celebrate the fact that He has taken His great power. It is a review of all that takes place and what follows when He appears out of heaven. The nations were full of wrath (Ps. ii; xlvi: 6); His wrath is come; resurrec-

tion will follow; this points to the time after the king-dom (chapter xx: 12). And His servants, the Prophets and the Saints, receive their reward, to reign with Him.

FOURTH DIVISION: SATAN'S POWER AND SATAN'S MASTERPIECE.
Chapter XI:19-XIII.

What follows now brings the great tribulation, the 1,260 days, into prominence. As we have seen the seventh trumpet takes us right to the end. But now we are led back.

Chapter XI. *1. The Vision of the Opened Temple. Verse 19.* This verse belongs properly to the twelfth chapter. The Ark contains the covenant made with Israel. This is now to be remembered and con-nected with it are the manifestations of coming wrath for those who oppress His people. God is now taking up the interests of His earthly people and as of old the Ark is the token of His presence with them and the coming victory.

Chapter XII. *2. The Woman with Child. Verses 1-2.* Who is represented by the Sun-clothed woman? Romanists have made out of her the Virgin Mary. Many expositors claim it is the Church which is repre-sented by this woman. Some claim the woman is the professing Church and the man-child represents, according to their view, a class of overcomers who will escape the tribulation. · This is a favored inter-pretation of some of the so-called "holiness people."

In the light of the scope of this book the woman cannot possibly have anything to do with the Church. Again, Christian Science has made the most absurd claim that this woman represents the instrument of Satan, the deluded woman, whom they worship as the founder of their cult. A hundred years ago another sect existed in England under the leadership of a woman, who also claimed to be the one of this vision. We do not need to seek long for the true meaning of the woman seen by John. She represents Israel.* Everything in the symbolical statements bears this out, especially the crown with the twelve stars (Gen. xxxvii:9).

"Thus she is seen clothed with the glory of the sun—that is, of Christ Himself as He will presently appear in supreme power as Sun of Righteousness (Mal. iv:2); for the sun is the ruler of the day. As a consequence, her glory of old, before the day-dawn, the reflected light of her typical system, is like the moon under her feet. Upon her head the crown of twelve stars speaks naturally of her twelve tribes, planets now around the central sun."

It is Israel, what she is in the purposes of God. And the child, the nation brought forth, is the Messiah, Christ. Even so Paul writes of Israel "of whom as according to the flesh Christ came, who is over all, God blessed forever (Rom. ix:5). The identity of the child is established beyond controversy by the fact that the child is caught up unto God and His throne, destined to rule all nations with a rod of iron (Ps. ii:9; Rev. ii:28). The great red Dragon, the

---

* Change "wonder" in 1 verse to "sign."

enemy of the woman and the child, is Satan. Seven
crowns are symbolical of his authority as the god of
this age and the ten horns symbolical of his power.
These historical facts are seen first through this vision.
But this is done for the one purpose of bringing into
view what is yet in store for Israel during the end time.
Christ ascended upon high, took His place at the right
hand of God, is waiting till His enemies are made His
footstool. Then the present Christian age began. It is
not recorded in this vision at all. He who came from
Israel and who was rejected by His own, is nevertheless Israel's Messiah, the Hope of Israel. In Him
and through Him alone the promises made to Israel
can be fulfilled. The fulfillment of these promises is
preceded by great sorrows and tribulation, the travail
pains which come upon Israel during the great tribulation, before He, whom Israel once disowned, is revealed as Deliverer and King. And the red Dragon
will do His most awful work during that period of
tribulation, a work of hatred against the faithful seed
of the woman.

3. *The Escape of the Woman. Verse 6.* The flight
of the woman, Israel, has been taken by some to mean
the dispersion of that nation during this age and
Israel's miraculous preservation. But that is incorrect.
It is true Israel has been miraculously preserved and
Satan's hatred too has been against that nation. But
here we have a special period mentioned, the 1,260
days, the last three and one-half years of Daniel's
seventieth week. It means therefore that when the

---

*It is Satan manifested or acting in the revived Roman
empire. Compare chap. xvii, 3.

Dragon rises in all his furious power to exterminate the nation, God will preserve her. However, before we are told the details of that preservation and Satan's hatred, we read of the war in heaven. Satan is cast out of heaven, down upon the earth. Verses 15-17 and the entire chapter xiii will tell us what he will do on the earth.

4. *War in Heaven and Satan Cast Out of Heaven. Verses 7-12.* This great scene takes place before the great tribulation begins. Satan's place is not in hell at this time. As we saw in the message to Pergamos his throne is on earth, he is the god of this age. His dominion is the air, he is the Prince of the power of the air (Eph. ii:2). Our present conflict as believers is "against principalities, against authorities, against the rulers of the darkness of this world, against the wicked spirits in the heavenlies" (Eph. vi:12). Satan as the accuser of the brethren has even access into the presence of God. The scene in Job i and ii is not a poetical invention, but presents a reality. He is still the accuser and our Lord Jesus Christ is our advocate. When the Saints are brought into glory they will not only behold the Lord Jesus Christ face to face, but, we believe Satan, that great fallen being, may also be seen by the Saints. The Lord will rebuke him (Zech. iii:2). His accusations are ended. All the redeemed are gathered before the throne. All the malice and power of Satan could not frustrate the purpose of God. His Grace and Power have been victorious. Thus when the Saints come into the heavenly possession Satan's dominion there is at an end. The purchased possession, the region above, will be re-

deemed by the power of God (Eph. i: 13). Michael and his angels will begin their short and decisive war against Satan and his angels. Michael is the one archangel mentioned in Scripture. It is not the first time he met Satan face to face. (Jude 9). And Daniel speaks of Michael, "And at that time shall Michael stand up, the great prince which standeth for the children of thy people; and there shall be a time of trouble, such as never was since there was a nation even to that same time; and at that time thy people shall be delivered, every one that shall be found written in the book" (Dan. xii: 1). From this we learn that Michael will not only cause the expulsion of Satan out of heaven, but he will also stand up for the believing portion of Israel.

Satan is then cast out into the earth and his angels are cast out with him. It is identical with what we have seen already under the fifth trumpet, the star fallen out of heaven, opening the pit of the abyss with the darkening smoke and the locust swarms coming forth. Then there is joy in heaven because the accuser is cast down and his accusations are forever silenced. And the "woe" is pronounced upon those who dwell on the earth.

5. *The Dragon Persecuting the Woman. Verses 13-17.* He turns in fury against the woman which brought forth the man child. Satan realizes now that his time is short. His expulsion from heaven will soon be followed by his arrest and imprisonment in the pit for a thousand years, and after that there is prepared for him his eternal home of misery, the lake of fire. As he knows that Israel is mostly concerned

in the final drama, and the believing portion of that nation will inherit the kingdom, he turns in wrath against them. Verse 6 should be connected with verse 14. It is symbolical language we have here again. The wilderness is a place of isolation, and the place prepared, speaks of God's care for them. But it is not the entire nation. The apostate part sides with Satan and with Satan's man, the Antichrist. But there is another part, which is preserved. This part is in the place of isolation among the nations. The water cast out by Satan is symbolical of the hatred which Satan stirs up against the people amongst the nations. These nations like Russia and others under Satanic control will persecute them. But there will be other agencies in the earth by which this Satanic attempt to wipe off the face of the earth this faithful part of the nation will be frustrated. These agencies will probably be those nations who have believed the final message, the Gospel of the Kingdom. Satan seeing himself defeated turns next against the godly remnant in the land itself (verse 17).

Chapter XIII. *The Beast Out of the Sea. Verses 1-10.* This chapter brings now fully into view the Satanic powers operating during the great tribulation —the forty-two months. Satan's masterpieces are on the earth; energized by him and endued with his powers they work together to stamp out all that is left of the truth on earth. Their combined efforts are directed against the godly remnant of Jews and against those Gentiles who accepted the message of the Gospel of the Kingdom, who are seen in the seventh chapter merging out of the great tribulation. They are called Beasts. The first is the revived Roman empire, which has over it a mighty leader. A careful study of Daniel's prophecy in chapter vii is here needed. The beast which John sees rising out of the sea is the Roman empire. This Daniel saw as a great nondescript, a dreadful beast with iron teeth and with ten horns. And John also sees this beast having ten horns* with crowns and seven heads and these heads had names of blasphemy. Daniel had seen Babylonia, Medo-Persia and Greco-Macedonia under the emblem of the lion, the bear and the leopard. John sees this beast here like a leopard, with bear's feet and lion's mouth. This revived Roman empire is an amalgamation of parts of the previous world empires. The preceding ones are absorbed by the last, the Roman empire. Therefore the revived Roman empire will contain the different elements in one great monster. This Roman empire will be revived in the first part of the final seven years. We saw this under the first seal. Here is the beginning of the forty-two months the Dragon gives to him his power, and his throne and great authority. It becomes now fully possessed by Satan. The ten horns are the ten kingdoms which will exist in that empire. We are told later that these ten kings "have one mind and shall give their power and strength unto the beast" (xvii: 13). In the same chapter the beast is also seen coming out of the abyss (xvii: 8) denoting its Satanic origin. The heads rep-

---

* The correct reading as given in the Revised Version is to put the horns first and the seven heads in the second place.

resent the seven forms of government which have characterized the empire in the past, the seventh becomes the eighth. One of the heads is especially mentioned; later we read "he is the eighth, and is of the seven, and goeth into perdition" (xvii: 11). It was as it were wounded to death, and his deadly wound was healed, and all the world wondered after the beast. This head denotes the imperial form of government, which had died, and now is revived in the person of the leader, the Prince of Daniel ix: 27, the little horn, which Daniel saw in the midst of the ten horns. This will be Satan's man, one of his masterpieces. The whole earth will wonder after that beast and its Satan possessed head.

"The Beast will represent a picture hitherto unknown and unseen—one unexampled in the history of the race. A human power endowed with Satanic energy—openly defying God, and invested with the royal power and world-wide authority of Satan—will engage the rapt gaze of the whole earth. It will marvel at the sight. We see no reason to limit the phrase 'the whole earth.' The revival of the empire must be a matter of interest to all embraced within its range and influence. The authority of the dragon, and his far-reaching influence go far beyond the geographical limits of the ten kingdoms. The beast to whom he delegates his authority, exercises a commanding influence all over the earth—reaching even to the limits of heathendom."*

Then when the head of the Beast has his Satanic power, the Dragon and the Beast are worshipped and

---

* W. Scott.

for the forty-two months he blasphemes and makes war with the Saints and overcomes them (the Jewish Saints). And he had power over all kindreds and tongues and nations. It is interesting to see that Daniel and Revelation agree perfectly in this matter. There is only this difference, Daniel describes mostly the head of the revived Roman empire, the little horn; John sees the empire as such. We quote the following from our book on Daniel:

Daniel	Revelation
Daniel saw the fourth beast, a great nondescript, with ten horns.	John beholds a beast out of the sea, with ten horns crowned (ten kings) and seven heads.
The little horn "had eyes and a mouth that spake very great things."	To the Beast "was given a mouth speaking great things and blasphemies."
The little horn: "He shall speak words against the Most High."	The Beast: "He opened his mouth in blasphemy against God."
The little horn: "He shall wear out the Saints of the Most High."	The Beast: "And it was given to him to make war with the Saints and to overcome them."
The little horn's time of domineering power is "a time and times and dividing of times."	The Beast has power for 42 months (3½ years).

"We see from this parallel that the same things are said of the Beast in Revelation xiii which are said of the little horn. They must therefore be identical. But how can we harmonize this if Revelation xiii, the Beast out of the sea, means the resurrected Roman empire? There lived a French King, Louis XIV, and in a famous speech he made the declaration 'I am France.' The little horn will possess such domineering powers, given to him by Satan, that he too can say 'I am the empire.' He will control the entire political sphere of the empire and thus gives to it his own Satanic God-defying character. In Daniel we see the same lesson, only in another setting."

7. *The Beast Out of the Earth. Verses 11-18.* The second Beast is not an empire with a great leader, but a person. The first Beast is out of the sea; the second out of the earth (land). The first has ten horns; the second has two. The Beast out of the sea comes first; the other Beast follows him. The first Beast is a political power; the second is a religious leader. The first is a Gentile power and its head a Gentile; the second is a Jew. The first Beast has Satanic power; so has the second Beast. The second Beast induced the worship of the first Beast whose dominion is over the entire Roman world and after whom the whole earth wanders; the sphere of the second Beast is Palestine. The first Beast through its head makes in the beginning of the seven years a covenant with many of the Jews, but in the middle of the week he breaks that covenant (Daniel ix: 27). That covenant will be probably the permission given to the Jews to build a temple and to resume their sacrificial worship. The first and the second Beast make a covenant, which marks the beginning of the seventieth week of Daniel. But when the little horn, the first Beast, becomes energized by Satan, he breaks that covenant. Then the second Beast demands the worship of the first Beast as well as the worship of himself. This second Beast is the final, personal Antichrist. He has two horns like a lamb, and speaks like

a dragon. He is a counterfeit lamb and his two horns
are an imitation of the priestly and kingly authority of
Christ. He is the one of whose coming our Lord spoke
(John v: 43). He is the man of sin, the son of perdition described by Paul in 2 Thess. ii. He must be a
Jew or his claim of being Israel's true Messiah would
not be accepted by the Jews. The view that he will
be Judas Iscariot raised from the dead is a fanciful
speculation. Daniel also gives an interesting prophetic
picture which bears out his Jewish character and his
wicked, satanic ways. See Daniel xi: 36-39. This
second Beast is also called the false Prophet (xvi: 13;
xix: 20; xx: 10). He does lying wonders. He reigns
as the false king in Jerusalem and sits as god in the
temple. He will be the religious head of apostate
Judaism and apostate Christendom. It is the strong
delusion of the second chapter of Second Thessalonians. He also demands the worship of the first Beast.
He makes an image of the first Beast and gives breath
to it, so that it can speak. Compare with the image
which Nebuchadnezzar set up (Daniel iii). This
image will most likely be put up outside of the land
of Palestine, perhaps in Rome, and in this way the
Beast will be worshipped. The most terrible persecution is connected with this idol-worship. The most
awful tyranny exists then, for all commerce is controlled by the Beast. Whosoever has not the mark of
the Beast on hand and forehead cannot buy nor sell,
and whosoever does not worship the Beast will be
killed. And those who worship the Beast and receive
the mark are lost souls. Great will be the number

of martyrs at that time. To find out what the mark is and some of the other details would only be guesswork. No one can imagine the horrors of that time when Satan rules for a short time on earth and produces the great tribulation, such as was not before on earth, nor ever can be again. May we praise God for His infinite Grace which saves us from that hour and may we reach out for those who, without Christ and without hope, are the subjects of this coming doom and eternal misery besides.

But what does the number 666 mean? If we were to state all the different views on this number and the different applications we would have to fill many pages and then we would not know what is right and wrong. Seven is the complete perfect number; six is incomplete and is man's number.* Here we have three times six. It is humanity fallen, filled with pride, defying God. The number 666 signifies man's day and man's defiance of God under Satan's power in its culmination.

FIFTH DIVISION. THE POWER OF GOD IN INTERVENTION. GRACE AND JUDGMENT MANIFESTED.

Chapter XIV.

1. The Lamb Upon Zion and the 144,000. Verses 1-5. A series of blessed visions follow the darkest chapter in the Book of Revelation. The awful condi-

---

* Six is the number of man. "Six days shalt thou labor." Six repeated three times is man fully manifested in evil.

tions under the domineering power of the two Beasts
are going to be changed. The Lord will answer the
prayers of the persecuted Jewish people and deliver
them by His personal coming out of the opened
heaven. This glorious manifestation is fully revealed
in the nineteenth chapter. Here it is anticipated.
There is much said about this intervention in behalf of
the suffering godly remnant in the Old Testament.
As an illustration we call attention to Psalms xliv and
xlv. In the forty-fourth Psalm we find a description
of their suffering and the cry to heaven "Arise for
our help, and redeem us for thy mercies sake." In the
forty-fifth Psalm the answer to this prayer is recorded.
The King riding in majesty, dealing with His enemies,
surrounded by redeemed companies is beheld in that
Psalm. The entire Book of Psalms should be studied
from the viewpoint of prophecy; it will shed much
light upon these events of this portion of Revelation.
But who are the 144,000 standing with the Lamb upon
Mount Zion, having His Name* and His Father's
Name written on their foreheads? In the previous
chapter we saw a company on earth who have the
mark of the Beast on their foreheads; but here is a
company who have His Name and the Father's Name
on the forehead. A good many have made of this
company a portion of the Church, a first fruits, who,
according to this theory, have lived separated lives
and are caught up into heaven, while the other believers, who did not live as near to God as they did,

* This has been unfortunately omitted in the Authorized
Version.

will have to suffer in the great tribulation. The reader who has followed the unfolding of this book will see at once that such an interpretation is impossible. These 144,000 have nothing to do whatever with the Church. The Elders are mentioned in verse 3 and as distinct from the 144,000, and, as we saw, the twenty-four Elders include and represent the Church. The 144,000 are the same company which was sealed in chapter vii, but they also include the distinctly Jewish remnant which suffered more specifically in Palestine. The number 144,000 being symbolical and not actual permits such an interpretation. In one word they represent the "all Israel" saved by the coming of the deliverer out of Zion (Rom. xi: 26). They have passed through the great tribulation and are seen as redeemed from the earth. And then there is heard the voice of harpers, making sweet music with their harps. They sing a new song (not as it were) before the throne and before the living creatures and the Elders. And the 144,000 learn to sing this new song. Who then are the harpers? They are the martyred company seen in connection with the fifth seal and they also include now their brethren which were slain during the great tribulation. The characteristics of the 144,000 are next given. Verse 4 must not be interpreted in a literal sense. Those who apply it to a first fruits of the church have done so and it has led to much confusion and even worse things. Literal impurity is not in view. If it had a literal meaning this company would consist of men only. The woman, the great harlot Bablyon and her daughters, the God-less and Christ-less religious world-systems (chapter xvii)

are then on earth. They did not defile themselves
with the corruptions and idolatries prevalent on the
earth. They kept themselves from spiritual fornication. They are the firstfruits and the earnest of the
blessings soon in store for the earth.* They were
devoted to the Lamb and no lie (not guile) was in
their mouth. The lie and delusion of the end-time were
utterly repudiated by them.

2. *The Proclamation of the Everlasting Gospel.*
Verses 6-7. This has nothing to do with the preaching
of the Gospel during this church-age. The Angel
must not be taken as a literal angel. The preaching
of any Gospel to those who dwell on earth is never
committed to angels, but to men. This is true of the
Gospel of Grace which redeemed sinners are privi-
leged to proclaim during this age, and of the everlasting Gospel during the end of the age. The Gospel
preached is the Gospel of the Kingdom and the preachers are this faithful remnant of God's earthly people.
Nothing of this preaching was said in chapter vii,
though the result, the gathered multitude coming out
of the great tribulation is seen there. But here, where
the moral and spiritual characteristics of the remnant
of Israel is seen, their testimony also comes into view.
What this everlasting Gospel is we need not explain

---

* The term firstfruits is also applied to true believers
constituting the Church (Rom. viii:23; 1 Cor. xv:20-22;
James i:18). We are the first fruits, the earnest of the
coming blessing for Israel and the nations. If the faithful remnant of Israel keeps itself undefiled from the religious
corruption of the end-time, how much more should we keep
ourselves as a separated people (2 Cor. vi:14; 2 Tim. ii:20-
21).

for verse 7 gives us the information. It is everlasting because it concerns the Creator as the only object of worship. And it will sound the loudest and go forth in no uncertain sound at the time when pandemonium reigns on earth, and heaven is about to open to manifest the King of Glory. How great is God's mercy! And the nations who hear and turn to God will enter the coming Kingdom. Read in connection with verses 6 and 7 Psalm xcvi. It will give you a great deal of light on this portion of Revelation.

3. Babylon has Fallen. Verse 8. This is an anticipative announcement of what will also happen as the great tribulation nears its close. The particulars are not given here. These and what Babylon is and how Babylon the great (city must be omitted in this verse) falls, we shall find in chapters xvii and xviii. God's intervention in judgment upon the great whore is simply mentioned here.

4. The Eternal Wrath for the Worshippers of the Beast. Verses 9-11. Here we have a third angelic announcement. It concerns the worshippers of the Beast. They drink of the wrath of God. It is "without mixture," that is, no mercy is found in the cup of His indignation. It serves as a solemn warning. Babylon falls prior to the glorious appearing of the King, and the Beast will afterward manifest his power as never before. Therefore, the warning concerning the inevitable fate of those who worship the Beast and take its mark. The warning cannot be twisted, though false teachers attempt it. It is Satan's deception, this increasing denial of the solemn truth of an everlasting, conscious and awful punishment of the wicked. By these denials, Satan prepares gradually, but surely, for the final great apostasy. "The smoke of their torment ascendeth forever and ever." There is no end to it. Unsaved reader! Be warned and accept Christ.

5. *The Blessed Dead Who Die in the Lord. Verses 12-13.* It is a voice which proclaims this. It refers especially to those who die as martyrs at that time. Certainly all our loved ones who fall asleep in Jesus are blessed. They are absent from the body and consciously present with the Lord. But here is the comfort for those who faithfully resist the worship of the Beast, who refuse to take the mark. They become martyrs. The Book of Revelation will be read and studied during the great tribulation. Satan through the Beasts, will try to annihilate it and the rest of the Bible. But it will be a failure as all former attempts to get the Bible out of the world have failed. Here then, is first the warning. If they worship the Beast they will be lost forever. Then there is the alternative to resist the Beast and be killed as to the body, but die in the Lord. "From henceforth" means during the tribulation when the great persecution goes on.

6. *The Harvest and the Vintage. Verses 14-20.* This brings now the Coming of the Son of Man with judgment power into view. The harvest and the vintage have come. The sickle is put in. The reapers used will be angels (Matt. xiii: 41). The day of vengeance has come. Read Isaiah lxiii: 1-6; Joel iii; Zechariah xii-xiv. This will greatly help to a better understanding of the harvest and the vintage. The

nations and their armies will be in the land; the Assyrian from the North, foreshadowed by the wicked work of Antiochus Epiphanes (Dan. viii) will do its awful work; the false prophet, the second Beast is in Jerusalem. But then the judgment clouds break. The battle of Armageddon comes into view for the first time in verse 20. How we ought to praise Him, for His infinite grace which has separated us from these awful judgments of vengeance and wrath. His people will be home when these things come to pass.

SIXTH DIVISION: THE SEVEN ANGELS HAVING THE SEVEN PLAGUES. THE VIALS OF WRATH.
Chapters XV-XVI.

Chapter XV. *1. The Seven Angels with the Seven Plagues. Verse 1.* And now the last seven angels appear. Seven seal judgments first, followed by seven angels with trumpets and next the last seven angels. With these seven angels who have the seven last plagues for the world, the wrath of God is completed. These great final manifestations of the wrath of God upon an apostate world are therefore conclusive. What wonderful order prevails in this book! What unfoldings of the future! What harmony with the previous portions of God's Word! Surely a human mind—a genius—could never have put these things together in this manner. It *is* revelation.

2. Another Scene of Worship. Verses 2-4. Before these angels go forth we behold another worship scene. Who are they? Not the twenty-four Elders, but they are the harpers which we saw harping and singing in chapter xiv: 2-3. They are the martyred company worshipping in glory. Here we are told of their victory and their song, the song of Moses and of the Lamb. The song of Moses (Exod. xv) is the song of an earthly deliverance and the song of the Lamb concerns a spiritual deliverance. They are redeemed by power and by blood.

3. The Seven Angels Proceeding out of the Temple. Verses 5-8. A wonderful sight it is. There is again an ominous silence similar to the silence in connection with the opening of the seventh seal. The silence is not mentioned. But the text shows an impressive scene of silence. Quietly the procession of these ministers of judgment file out of the temple. They are clothed in pure, white linen; this is symbolical of the righteousness which demands the judgment wrath about to be poured out. And the golden girdles with which their breasts are girdled speak still more of divine righteousness. God in His righteousness must judge and now His wrath in completeness is about to be felt on the earth. The angels left the temple empty-handed, but the four living creatures give into their hands the bowls full of the wrath of God. And behind that smoke is the fire of judgment. He is hidden in the thick darkness of His Glory (Exod. xix: 18; Ps. xviii: 8; Isaiah vi: 4).

Chapter XVI. *4. The First Vial. Verses 1-2.* The great voice commands the seven angels to go on their way and to empty the bowls upon the earth (Ps. lxix: 24). And these vials of judgments affect not only the Roman empire, but the entire world, for the whole world is guilty before God. The first

vial poured out produces a grievous sore upon the
worshippers of the Beast. While it is undoubtedly
true that we have symbols also in these vial judgments, it is nevertheless possible that some of these
plagues may have, besides the symbolical, also a
literal meaning. The sixth plague which came upon
Egypt, the first judgment upon the persons of the
Egyptians, was also a sore (Exod. ix: 10-11). The
worshippers of the Beast and of the image will be
dreadfully afflicted. All the internal corruption will
be outwardly manifested. There will be connected
with it great agony and suffering; and as a sore is a
vile thing to behold, we may think of the great vileness
connected with the moral, apostate conditions in the
earth, which God will permit to break out.

5. *The Second Vial. Verse 3.* This is poured out
into the sea. The sea represents the Gentiles. These
will now experience the wrath of God. See the plague
in Egypt (Exod. vii: 17-25.) That was a literal thing;
but not so here. Some apply it to the continued carnage which will be one of the leading features of the
final history of the times of the Gentiles. That it
presents a state of the most unspeakable corruption
and spiritual death is obvious. How little we can say
of all these awful scenes of wrath coming upon the
earth. It is far better to acknowledge our ignorance
in some of these matters than to indulge in fanciful
speculations.

6. *The Third Vial. Verses 4-7.* Another scene
in which the blood is prominent. The Apostates denied the blood, sneered at it as the Unitarians and
Christian Scientists do in our own days, and now the

angel of the waters saith, "Thou hast given them blood to drink, for they are worthy." They have to feel the dreadful results of having rejected the Christ of God and accepted the man of sin. The children of Israel had to taste their own idolatry when Moses put the ashes of the burnt golden calf in the water and made them drink it (Exod. xxxii: 20). They have to taste the vileness and bitterness of their apostasy. They reap what they sow. All the joys of life typified by rivers and fountains of water, are poisoned and corrupted. It is a retributive judgment of God falling then upon the earth.

7. *The Fourth Vial. Verses 8-9.* The fourth vial is poured into the sun and men are scorched with great heat. Some also apply this literally, but the symbolical meaning is to be preferred. There can be no doubt but the powers of nature will also bear witness to the wrath of God. Famines, droughts, great floods, volcanic disturbances, great and widespread earthquakes and other physical phenomena will occur throughout these days of tribulation. However, the sun here is not the physical sun, but means, as under the fourth trumpet, the supreme authority governing them (the Roman empire). Under the fourth trumpet great moral darkness came upon all; here it is fearful, fiery agony "scorched with great heat." The government, Satan-ruled as it is, becomes now the source of the most awful torment to those who are under its dominion. God, in judgment and in His wrath, permits those terrible things to come to pass. Everything under these vial judgments will become more aggravated than under the trumpet judgment.

And what will those do who are drinking the cup of wrath? They do not repent, but blaspheme. What an evidence of their hopeless condition!

8. *The Fifth Vial. Verses 10-11.* Under the fifth trumpet we saw the star fallen from heaven. It synchronizes with chapter xii: 7-12—Satan cast out of heaven. Then Satan fallen from heaven gave his power and authority to the Beast, the head of the empire. Here the throne (not seat) of the Beast is dealt with. His throne and his kingdom is deluged with wrath. All becomes darkness.* The boast had been "Who is like unto the Beast? Who is able to make war with him?" (xiii: 4). Here God answers this boast with wrath. Then they begin to gnaw their tongues with pain. However, it is not yet the complete judgment of the two Beasts. That comes later.

9. *The Sixth Vial. Verse 12.* Once more the river Euphrates is mentioned. It dries up when the sixth bowl is poured out so that the way of the kings of the East (literal: from the rising of the sun) might be prepared. We have hinted before at the correspondence between the trumpet judgments and the pouring out of the vials. This becomes now very marked, for under the sixth trumpet the river Euphrates is also mentioned. There the forces which keep back hostile powers are removed and here the river is dried up. The historical interpretation is responsible for the theory that the Euphrates is Turkey. But is there anything in Revelation which would warrant the interpretation that this river means Turkey? We know nothing whatever. If the Euphrates really

---

*See the judgment plague upon Egypt (Exod. x: 21-23).

meant the Turkish power then the drying up of the river has been going on for a number of decades. But here it is not a gradual thing but a sudden event. Nor does this event take place as long as the true Church is here, but after the Church is removed. As already stated the Euphrates was the boundary of the Roman empire and the land of Israel. It is a kind of barrier which separates the West from the East. This barrier symbolized by the river Euphrates is now completely removed, so that the kings from the sunrise can invade the land. This invasion is also seen in connection with the sixth trumpet. The nations must gather from all quarters in and about Palestine. We find much of this revealed in the Old Testament and it would be strange if the Revelation were silent on so important an event. Ezekiel describes a great invader, a confederacy of nations (Ezek. xxxviii and xxxix). Gog, Magog, the Prince of Rosh* (Russia), Meshech, Tubel, Persia, Cush and Put are mentioned as forming this confederacy. The term "Kings of the sunrise" may even mean the far Eastern Asiatic nations, like China and Japan. We hear much of "the yellow peril" in our day. The drying up of the Euphrates seems therefore to mean the removal of the barrier, so that the predicted gathering of the nations may take place (Joel iii:2). What began under the sixth trumpet is consummated when the sixth vial is poured out. It is an act of judgment-wrath, while at the same time these opposing nations are gathering for the great day of God Almighty.

---

* This is the correct translation of "chief prince."

*Between the Sixth and Seventh Vial. A Paren-
thetical Vision. Verses 13-16.* Just as we had a
parenthetical vision between the sixth and seventh
seal, and between the sixth and seventh trumpet, so
we find here a very brief one between the sixth and
seventh vial judgment. Armageddon is not yet, but
it comes now in view. Unclean spirits, like frogs,
creatures of the slimy, evil-smelling swamps and of
the night, now proceed out of the mouth of the trinity
of evil. The Dragon is Satan; the Beast the political
head of the empire and the false Prophet, the Anti-
christ. Satanic influences, emanating from him and
his two master-pieces are then at work; and they are
of such a nature that we cannot fully understand them.
They are the spirits of demons, working miracles.
Doctrines of seducing spirits and demons, like Christian Science, Spiritism and Theosophy are already in
the world. They are Satan's instruments. But when
the three unclean spirits come forth it will be far
worse. It is a judgment also. Compare with 1 Kings
xxii: 13-23. The kings are gathered for the battle
which is to come. And it is God Himself who does
this gathering. What will happen when they are
gathered we see in chapter xix. A final warning is
given of His coming.

10. *The Seventh Vial. Verses 17-21.* The seventh
angel pours his vial into the air. This is Satan's
sphere. His power and dominion is now dealt with in
wrath. While Satan was cast out of heaven, he may
still maintain part of the atmosphere immediately
above the earth, thus upholding his claim as the prince
of the power of the air (Eph. ii:2). A great voice

declares "It is done." All that follows shows that the climax is reached. The judgment shown is sweeping everything. A great earthquake as under the sixth seal and the seventh trumpet takes place. The great city Bablyon is divided into three parts; the cities of the nations fall. It is the hour of collapse, when the stone from above does its smiting work (Dan. ii). "It is done!" The Lord has come. The nineteenth chapter will furnish us the particulars.

SEVENTH DIVISION. THE GREAT HARLOT BABYLON AND HER JUDGMENT.
Chapters XVII-XVIII.

Chapter XVII. *1. The Description of the Woman. Verses 1-6.* Babylon was mentioned for the first time in this book in chapter xiv:8; her fall was then anticipated. In two chapters we have a description of her and the details of her overthrow and complete destruction. Babylon is seen as a great, world-wide ecclesiastical, political and commercial system, and her dwelling place, from where she exercises authority, is a great city, which is the seven-hilled city Rome. There are many who believe that the literal Babylon is in view here in these two chapters. It is claimed that literal Babylon on the banks of the Euphrates is to become once more a large city and the seat of government during the end of this age. Literal Babylon never was a part of the Roman empire, and as the Babylon of Revelation xvii and xviii is seen in closest identification with the empire, and for a time at least is its center and capital, the Babylon in Asia is ruled out at once. Rome was the great center of the Roman

empire and Rome will once more become the seat
where the woman pictured in this chapter will exercise her authority. We fully believe, however, that
ancient Babylon will also be rebuilt. One only needs
to turn to Isaiah xiii: 20-22 to find the proof of that.
Such a destruction of literal Babylon has never been.
Babylon at the present time is quite an influential
town and constantly growing. Great irrigation
schemes and railroads are planned for Mesopotamia.
When Euphrates comes into prominence, as we have
seen under the sixth trumpet and the sixth vial, and the
invasion from the far East, from the "sun-rise" takes
place, there must needs arise on the banks of the
Euphrates the ancient city and become a city of
prominence once more. Then after that her final
destruction will come. See Jeremiah li. All this is
clear and cannot be denied. But it is equally clear
that the Babylon described in these two chapters in
Revelation is not the literal Babylon.

In the first part of this chapter we have a description
of the great harlot Babylon. Who then is this woman,
branded a harlot, which one of the seven angels who
poured out the vials showed to John? She represents
the Papal system in its final power and control in the
world. We shall see how this assertion is fully con-
firmed by the words of this chapter. We saw in the
church-message to Thyatira, which stands for the
Papacy and its great corruption, that Rome is pictured
as the woman Jezebel, corresponding to the woman in
the parable of the leaven. And of Thyatira it is
said "she repents not." This shows that Rome will
continue in her corrupt ways to the end, till judg-

ment overtakes her. She is to be cast into great tribulation (ii: 22). When the true Church is caught up, the Papal system, as we call it, the Roman Catholic "church" will see a great revival. For a time she has been stripped of the temporal power she once had, but it will be restored to her. Along with the revival of the Roman empire there will be a revival of Papal Rome. Indications of this are numerous at the present time. While we see the possible European Confederacy looming up, culminating in the resurrected empire, we see also that Rome will soon see her revival. Many voices are heard in Protestantism suggesting a union with Rome, thus producing a great "world-church," a strange and significant term. This present war must end some day and we should not at all be surprised if the man, who claims to be "the head of the church on earth," will play an important part when peace is made. The negotiations for peace may be made in the city of Rome. But we must look very briefly at some of the descriptions of this woman, the harlot. "She sitteth upon many waters." We find the interpretation in verse 15. "The waters which thou sawest, where the whore sitteth are peoples, and multitudes, and nations and tongues." Rome even now can boast of her children among all nations. She gets her support from the whole world. And when she gets her revival she will have a still greater dominion. The kings of the earth then yield once more to her spiritual fornication. Then John saw the woman upon a scarlet colored beast, full of names of blasphemy, having seven heads and ten horns. Who is the Beast she rides? It is the first Beast of chapter

xiii, the revived Roman empire. She becomes identified with that empire. Her attire is in purple, scarlet
and she is decked with gold and precious stones and
pearls. The Pope and his Cardinals wear these colors.
Purple and scarlet are the leading colors displayed in
great Romish celebrations. And gold, precious stones
and pearls describe her enormous wealth and dazzling
glory, so attractive to the natural man. And in her
hand was a golden cup full of abominations and
filthiness of her fornication. How clearly this describes Papal Rome. Her service, called worship,
her rituals, her splendid edifices, etc., all is fair to
behold and pleasing to the eye, like a golden cup. But
inside we find her filthiness in doctrine and in prac-
tices. She encourages sin by her indulgences. With
the celibacy there is also filth connected. And then
the vileness and abomination of the confessional. Her
shameless character is written upon her forehead. The
true Church is to have His name upon the forehead
and the great harlot-system bears also an inscription.
"Mystery" is the first word. It has been well put by
another:

"Her name is Mystery, yet it is written on her forehead.
Her character is plain, if only you can read it. If you are
pure, you may soon know that she is not. If you are
true, you may quite easily detect her falsehood. In lands
where she bears sway, as represented in this picture, she
has managed to divorce morality from religion in such a
manner that all the world knows the width of the breach.
Her priests are used to convey the sacraments; and one
need not look at the hands too closely that do so needful
a work. In truth, it is an affair of the hands, with the
magic of a little breath by means of which the most sinful
of His creatures can create the God that made him, and

easily new-create, therefore, another mortal like himself. This is a great mystery, which she herself conceives as "sacrament," and you may see this clearly on her forehead then. It is the trick of her trade, without which it could not exist. With it, a little oil and water and spittle become of marvelous efficacy (the wafer in the mass) her capital stock indeed, out of which, at the smallest cost, the church can create riches and power, and much that has unquestionable value in her eyes."*

And she is "Babylon the Great." Babylon means confusion; it is the great confusion, all the evils and perversions of the truth of God brought into one powerful organization. And she is the mother of all harlots and abominations of the earth. Every religious system which aims at worldly power and grandeur and which shares more or less her assumptions and false doctrines is one of her offsprings. These systems, after the restraining power of the Holy Spirit is gone, will naturally unite with "mother church" and form the great Babylon.† And she was drunken with the blood of the Saints and with the blood of the martyrs of Jesus, so that John wondered with a great wonder. Such were her cruel, wicked, Satanic deeds in the past.

The inquisition, the torture-chambers, the countless victims who were burned to death and cruelly tortured, the unspeakable horrors of centuries of violence and murder come to our mind as we read this description.

---

* Numerical Bible.

† A good part of the "Church of England" is ready to unite with Rome. Leading Protestant preachers have also said that Christendom should soon unite and acknowledge Rome.

It could never be true of the literal Babylon. Nor does it mean, as Romish expositors of this book claim, pagan Rome, for if it meant the persecutions under the Roman Emperors, John would not have wondered with a great wonder. And the last page of her cruel, horrible, persecutions is not yet written. When she comes in power again, she will do the same thing, enabled, no doubt, by the power of the Beast. Papal Rome, the blood-thirsty, corrupt system is what we see here and Rome is seen in her coming revival.

2. *The Interpretation by the Angel. Verses 7-15.* The interpreting angel told John who the Beast is, the Beast, that was, and is not, and yet is (verse 8). It is the Roman empire, as stated before. It was, in an imperial form in John's day. In the fifth century, A.D., it ceased existing as imperial Rome; it is not. But it is to be again, a revival which is here described as coming out of the pit of the abyss (chapter xiii). Verse 9 shows Rome (seven mountains)* where the woman sitteth. Therefore Rome speaks of "the See of the Papacy," and "See" is derived from the Latin *Sedes,* which means seat or throne.

The seven kings or heads in verse 10 mean different forms of government of the Roman empire. Five are fallen; these were Kings, Consuls, Dictators, Decemvirs and Military Tribunes. These are past forms of government. But in John's day the empire had the imperial form of government. This is the meaning of "one is." The other and final form of the Roman empire "is not yet come." That is in John's day

---

* Romans call the seven hills upon which "the eternal city"—so-called, is built *Montes*—mountains.

it had not yet come. It is the Satanic revival and control of the empire as we saw it in chapter xiii. And
the eighth head, which goeth into perdition, is the man
who heads the empire, the little horn, which Daniel saw
on the ten-horned Beast. The ten horns in verses
12-13 are the kings. They correspond to the ten
toes on Nebuchadnezzar's image and the ten horns
on the fourth Beast which Daniel saw coming out of
the sea. And these ten kings yield their power and
strength unto the Beast. In verse 14, their awful
future is seen. We shall see this more fully in chapter
xix: 11-21. They are going to make war with the
Lamb, and the Lamb, who is Lord of lords and King
of kings, will overcome them. With Him are the
called, the chosen and the faithful, that is the redeemed, who come with Him and are manifested when
He appears.

3. *The Desolation of the Whore. Verses 16-18.*
The woman rides the Beast for a short time only.
She will not be long successful in her regained power.
The ten horns, the ten kingdoms, and the Beast*
hate her and turn against the whore. First they
were all for her and now they unite in making her
desolate and naked and burn her with fire. But
more than that "and shall eat her flesh," just as
Jezebel was eaten by the dogs. It is God in His
righteous judgment who decreed her desolation in this
way. "And the woman which thou sawest is that

---

* "And the Beast" is not in the authorized version; it is
added in the Revised Version and belongs rightfully into
the text.

great city, which reigneth over the kings of the earth."
The City is none other than Rome.

Chapter XVIII. *4. The Angelic Announcement.*
Verses 1-3. Babylon is now seen under another
aspect. In the former chapter we have the religious
center of Rome and her wicked idolatries, in the
present chapter it includes also the whole system of
apostate Christendom in its social and commercial aspect, the so-called "Christian civilization" in its final
apostate condition and doom. Papal Rome in her
short revival becomes the head of apostate Christendom and controls everything till her appointed
doom comes upon her. While we saw in the preceding
chapter the desolation of the whore by the ten kings
and the Beast, here we see how God views her and that
He dethrones this system by His judgment. A strong
angel comes down to announce her doom and to lay
bare her inner and most awful corruption. A strong
descending Angel* whose glory lightened the earth,
shows what the boasting thing, she, who bore the
blessed name of Christ, has become. She is seen to be
the habitation of demons. Even now behind all the
denials of the doctrine of Christ and the false doctrines
which mark the onward march of the predicted apostasy, demons are the leaders (1 Tim. iv: 1). But what
will it be when the demons are in full power on the
earth and all Christendom has joined itself to the

---

* This angel may represent the Lord Himself. If this is
correct we have the third manifestation of our Lord in the
garb of an angel. viii: 3 in His priestly dignity; x: 1 in His
royal dignity and here as the herald and executor of the
vengeance of God upon Babylon.

Romish whore! That great "world-church" has become "the hold of every foul spirit, and a cage of every unclean and hateful bird." The mustard tree parable (Matthew xiii) points out this also. The birds which flock into the branches are unclean things. Christendom has been this in the past and it is now, but when at last all is united with Rome and forms one vast ecclesiastical system, then every foul spirit, every unclean and hateful bird will be found in her. And the nations drank eagerly her cup and the kings committed fornication with her. These kings are not the ten kings of the Empire for they are used in the judgment of the whore, while the kings mentioned here bewail her destruction (verse 9). And with the system there was connected great commerce; merchants through her became rich.

5. The Call to Separate. Verses 4-5. God always calls out His true children from that which is evil. His own must be a separate people. Saints in past centuries have heard this call and left behind the Romish abominations and thousands sealed their testimony with their blood. And in these days in which our lot is cast, days with increasing signs, heralding as never before the approaching end and the home-call of His people to meet Him in the air, in these days God demands the separation of His true children. Christendom is becoming daily more and more the religious camp of apostasy. And therefore He calls "Let us go forth unto Him without the camp bearing His reproach" (Heb. xiii: 13). He who remains in that which denies His Name, is partaker of her sins (verse 4 compare with 2 John, verses 10-11).

As all drifts back to Rome and the coming political and religious confederacy, this final Babylon looms up, God's people must hear that call. And what shall we say of certain professional evangelists who instead of sounding this divine call, laud Rome, speak well of her, so that their supposed "converts" unite with the Romish whore by the hundreds! But there is to be a final call to come out of her, after the true Church is gone. To whom is this call addressed? Undoubtedly to the remnant of God's ancient people, the believing remnant* and also to that large number of Gentiles who hear the final message, the Gospel of the Kingdom.

6. *Her Pride and Righteous Destruction. Verses 6-8.* The language of righteous retribution used in the sixth verse reminds of Psalm cxxxvii: 8. "O daughter of Babylon, thou shalt be destroyed; happy shall he be that rewardeth thee as thou hast served us." It is the language not of Christians, who are exhorted not to recompense evil for evil, but of the remnant of Israel. Like ancient Babylon, the whole apostate system, Rome and all her offsprings, was filled with pride. She was lifted up in all her earthly glory and now God breaks her completely. "She shall be utterly burned with fire." As her smoke is to arise forever and ever (xix: 3) it is possible that the proud city, Rome, the center of the system of apostasy and commerce will be destroyed by volcanic action, and where the seven-hilled city once stood there may be instead an immense crater, testifying throughout the millennium of God's righteous retribution. In view of

---

*Jeremah li: 6 concerns the literal Babylon of the past. Godly Jews were exhorted to flee her.

the volcanic conditions on the Italian peninsula this is more than possible. Rome means "strong," but her strength will be broken when the strong Lord God judgeth her. The judgment which Babylon executed on God's people is now executed upon Babylon.

7. *The Universal Lamentation Over Her. Verses 9-19.* And now follows the great and universal lamentation over the destruction of the great world-system. There is weeping and wailing when at last this Antichristian civilization, all Christendom united with Rome, and for a time controlling the commerce of the world, is wiped out by the hand of God. The kings, the merchants, the shipmasters, the company in ships and sailors, all are seen mourning, weeping and wailing. The destruction of the system and of its proud city affects them all. They bewail their great loss. Notice twenty-eight things are mentioned by them. The first is gold and the last the souls of men. How this describes Rome! She is the trafficker in souls and the destroyer of souls as well. And in studying the articles of the commerce of apostate Christendom we notice that these are nearly all articles of luxury. The greatest panic has then come and there will be no recovery of the market. The rich men will weep and howl for their misery is come upon them (James v: 1). See also Zeph. i: 11, 18.

8. *The Rejoicing Heavens. Verse 20.* Heaven is called to rejoice over her and three classes are mentioned (Revised Version) Saints, Apostles and Prophets. "For God hath judged your judgment on her." This is the better rendering. The judgment which the

saints pronounced on her is now executed. The next chapter shows us more fully the rejoicing heavens.

9. Her Utter and Everlasting Destruction. Verses 21-23. In Jeremiah li: 60-64 we read that Seraiah was commissioned by Jeremiah to attach a stone to the book containing the prophet's words and to cast it into the Euphrates. "And thou shalt say, thus shall Babylon sink and shall not rise from the evil that I will bring upon her and they shall be weary." Here an angel took up a millstone and cast it into the sea showing by this action the complete and final destruction of the wicked system and the equally wicked city. And what revelation there is in the statement "for by thy sorceries were all nations deceived." In chapter xx we read that the old Serpent deceives the nations. Sorceries, wicked spirits, demon-powers blinded the eyes of the nations to follow Rome's seductive lure. And thus it is with a life-less, spirit-less Protestantism and its blood-less Gospel. The sorceries of Rome, the demons underneath it all, attract apostate Christendom so that all will be united in the great, final Babylon.

10. The Blood of the Saints Found in Her. Verse 24. So that we may not err that both chapters refer to Rome, though the entire Apostate Christendom is also in view, her blood-guiltiness is mentioned once more. Chapter xvii: 6.*

---

* Alas! she has erected the prisons, and prepared the rack, and lighted the fires of what she calls the holy office of the Inquisition in Italy, Spain, America, and India. She lauds one of her canonized Popes, Pius the Fifth, in her Breviary, as an inflexible Inquisitor. She has engraven the massacre of St. Bartholomew's Day on her Papal coins, and

EIGHTH DIVISION. THE MANIFESTATION OF THE KING AND THE MILLENNIUM.

Chapters XIX-XX: 16

We reach the great climax in this wonderful book. The King in His glorious majesty is now to be manifested to deal with the earth in the great judgment and to receive the throne which is promised unto Him. The seven years of darkness, apostasy and tribulation, the years in which man's day reached its awful culmination, the years of manifestation of demon powers which produced the greatest wickedness and blasphemy the earth has seen, are about over. The Lamb of God, the Lion of the tribe of Judah executed the decreed judgments from above. The seals of the book He received were opened by Him. The angels have blown their judgment trumpets and the things written have come to pass. The other seven angels have poured out their vials upon the earth. The beginning of sorrow was followed by the great tribulation. Political and ecclesiastical upheavals indescribable have taken place. The great nations formed their confederacy, the revived Roman empire, and Satan put his man, the little horn, at the head of the empire. Out of Israel's land and in the midst of that land the second Beast arose, the false prophet, the false Messiah. These two Satan possessed instruments, as we saw, worked together and through them and other agencies, Satan, cast out of heaven, produced the great

---

there represents it as a work done by an angel from heaven. And the Roman Pontiff of that day went publicly to Church to return thanks to God for that savage and treacherous deed.—*Wordsworth.*

tribulation. In the midst of all these terrible scenes of bloodshed, revolution and indescribable confusion the remnant of Israel gave their faithful testimony, while the remnant in the land suffered and thousands of these faithful witnesses were martyred, because they refused to worship the Beast and to receive the mark of the Beast. And a great multitude of Gentiles were saved through the preaching of the Gospel of the kingdom, which they heard from the sealed remnant of Israel. Then we saw Babylon, the final ecclesiastical condition of apostate Christendom, headed by Rome in a world-wide system, and we saw the fall and total destruction of the city and the system. The end of the seven years has come and heaven is now to speak and the King with His heavenly company, the Saints and also His angels, is about to appear crowned with many crowns. The King is about to come, for the great day of God Almighty, when He, as the executor of the day of vengeance, is to tread the winepress of the fierceness and wrath of Almighty God.

Before we enter upon the exposition of this great and long-predicted event, the visible and glorious coming of our Lord, let us picture briefly the conditions on earth when the heavens are about to open and He comes back. No human being, however, can do that fully, for the conditions and scenes which will exist then beggar description. In the previous chapter we heard the wail and lamentation over the destruction of the great Babylon. They cast dust on their heads and there was weeping and wailing (xviii: 19). These lamentations over the loss of earthly prosperity, over the destruction of the great ecclesiastical and

commercial system will continue. But there is
greater fear than that. The approaching day is felt
by all. What we saw under the sixth seal is now
being fully enacted. The fulfillment of the words
of our Lord in Luke xxi:25-27 is at hand. "And
there shall be signs in the sun, and in the moon, and
in the stars; and upon the earth distress of nations
with perplexity; the sea and the waves roaring; men's
hearts failing them for fear, and for looking after
those things which are coming on the earth, for the
powers of the heavens shall be shaken. And then shall
they see the Son of Man coming in a cloud with power
and great glory." While such fear takes hold upon
the people and the terror of the coming Lord is upon
them, the Beast, that is the head of the Roman empire, and the kings of the earth with him, take another attitude. They become under Satanic leadership
so darkened and possessed that they rush towards the
land of Israel. The defiance pictured in the Second
Psalm has reached its climax. Besides this the great
gathering from beyond the Euphrates under the leadership of the King of the North and the Kings from
the Sunrise has taken place. The northern and eastern
hordes sweep into the land and threaten the Beast and
the Kings with him. The nations are massed with
their armies in Palestine. In Jerusalem the greatest
distress prevails. The second Beast, the Anti-christ,
called also the false Prophet, has his seat there, and as
we saw in the eleventh chapter as well as in the thir-
teenth, large numbers of the faithful Jewish remnant
are slain by him. The city is surrounded by the hostile
armies and the siege described by Zechariah is taking

place. And those who endure to the end and hold
out against the false Messiah (Matt. xxiv) pray as
never before and call for heaven's intervention. Their
prayer will be "Oh that Thou wouldest rend the
heavens and come down" (Is. lxiv: 1). It is then when
the nations rage and Satan's power is at its height
that the answer comes from above. The earth shakes
in its very foundations and now the powers of the
heavens also begin to shake. The ominous signs in
the Sun, in the Moon and in the Stars are seen. The
fact that something startling is about to happen from
above is realized by the Beast, and the kings with their
armies. Then the Beast, the kings of the earth and
their armies, utterly blinded by Satan, are ready to
make war against Him who is about to be manifested.
No doubt their well-equipped aeroplanes and other air-
crafts circle upward to interfere with the coming King
and His army. Then the blow falls upon them. The
stone, which Nebuchadnezzar saw falling out of
heaven, strikes at last and the Son of Man appears
in the clouds of heaven to take the kingdom. We
must now look at the details of this great revelation.

Chapter XIX. *1. The Four Hallelujahs in Heaven.
The Marriage of the Lamb. Verses 1-10.* Once more
we find the significant phrase "after these things"
(chapter iv: 1; vii: 1; xviii: 1). "After these things"
—the things which are described in chapters xvii and
xviii, the fall of Babylon and the complete destruction
of the whore and the system over which she presided
and domineered, after these things, voices in heaven
are heard again. We were first introduced to the
heavens in this book in the fourth chapter. Then

a door was opened in heaven, symbolical of the entrance of the Saints of God of all ages into glory. It is the fulfillment of 1 Thess. iv: 13-18. Then we saw what transpired in glory. All the Saints, God's redeemed people gathered around the throne and occupying thrones worshipping and singing the song of redemption. Under the fifth seal we had another glimpse of heaven. The first martyred company, the souls under the altar cried with a loud voice, How long O Lord? And they received their white robes. Then we read of silence in heaven and saw the Angel-Priest in His ministration at the altar (viii: 1-5) while in the tenth chapter we beheld Him descending out of heaven. The martyred Saints during the tribulation we saw, raised from the dead and taken in the cloud into heaven (xi: 12) while immediately after, when the seventh angel trumpeted, the heavens were celebrating in worship and in praise the consummation reached and the coming reign of the King. Again in the twelfth chapter we saw the rejoicing heavens. They that dwell in them rejoiced because the accuser of the brethren was cast down, and knowing what it means for the earth when Satan is there, the heavens pronounced their woe. In chapter xiv we beheld the heavens again, the redeemed company praising as well as the harpers. Chapter xv revealed another heavenly scene. Babylon's fall was also known to the tenants of heaven. This brief review is to show that while these things are going on in the earth, the glorified Saints, we His people who will then be in His presence, will know, and not be ignorant of the events on earth. We shall see them all from above and praise

Him for His grace which saved us and brought us to glory.

In chapter xviii: 20 we heard the words addressed to heaven "Rejoice over her, thou heaven, and ye holy apostles and prophets, for God hath avenged you on her." And now we see heaven rejoicing. "I heard as it were* a great voice of a great multitude in heaven saying "Hallelujah." Hallelujah means "Praise ye Jehovah." This Hebrew word is not found elsewhere in the New Testament. Four times this word of praise is found in the beginning of this chapter; the Hallelujah times for heaven and earth are imminent. The Book of Psalms closes with many Hallelujahs; the blessed time which the Psalms so often anticipate, when the earth is judged in righteousness and the glory of the Lord is manifested, is now at hand. The praise here is on account of the righteousness of God exhibited in the judgment of the great whore "which did corrupt the earth with her fornication" and because the blood of God's servants shed by her is now avenged. The great multitude whose Hallelujah is heard first must be the company of martyrs who died during the tribulation. The souls under the altar and their brethren which were slain later utter this praise now. They are seen as a distinct company from the twenty-four Elders. A second Hallelujah is uttered by them, while the smoke of the destroyed city goes up forever and ever. "And the four and twenty Elders and the four living Creatures fell down and worshipped God that sitteth on the

---

* Revised Version.

throne, saying, Amen, Hallelujah." The whole redeemed company, Old and New Testament Saints, add
their Amen and Hallelujah to the outburst of praise
on account of the execution of the righteous judgment.
And they worship God for it is His righteousness
which accomplished the destruction of the great whore.
In the midst of this wonderful and impressive worship-
scene the throne begins to be heard. A voice from the
throne said "Give Praise unto God all ye His servants
and ye that fear Him both small and great." And the
command is at once obeyed. John hears the fourth
Hallelujah and it is the greatest, the most mangnificent.
It is the great Hallelujah-chorus of heaven. Like the
voice of many, roaring waters, like the voice of mighty
thunderings a great multitude saith "Hallelujah for the
Lord our God Omnipotent reigneth." Who is this
great multitude? In the first verse we heard the Hallelujah of the martyred companies. The twenty-four
Elders and four living Creatures did not join in this
first Hallelujah. Their Hallelujah followed. And now
the great outburst of a great multitude. This multitude includes all the redeemed in glory. And they
rejoice and give glory for an additional reason which
is made known for the first time in this book. The
marriage of the Lamb is about to be consummated.
"Let us be glad and rejoice, and give honor to Him,
for the marriage of the Lamb is come and His wife has
made herself ready." The harlot, which claimed to be
the bride, being judged, the true bride of Christ is
seen in glory. And it is the marriage of the Lamb.
His joy is now filled full for He receives her, who is
bone of His bone and flesh of His flesh. The second

Man, the last Adam, is joined to her who is to rule
and reign with Him. But who is the bride about to
become the Lamb's wife? Some teach that it is Israel
to be united with the Lord in the closest bonds. But
these expositors forget that the scene is a heavenly
one. This marriage does not take place on earth where
the faithful remnant looks up expecting Him to appear
for their deliverance, but this marriage is in glory. It
is true such relationship is declared to be Israel's in the
Old Testament. She was married to Jehovah in a legal
covenant and on account of her faithless condition,
because Jerusalem played the harlot (Ezek. xvi: 35)
she was put away. For a time Israel was the wife
of Jehovah (Is. liv: 1) and then on account of her
wickedness became divorced. She will be taken back
in the day of her national repentance when the Lord
comes. But as one who had been divorced she cannot be a bride again. The bride of Christ to become
the Lamb's wife is the Church of the New Testament.
All who accepted Christ as Saviour and Lord since the
day of Pentecost constitute the bride of Christ. The
Church began on Pentecost and her completion will
be the translation to glory (1 Thess. iv: 17). She is
both the body of Christ and the bride of Christ, as
Eve was of the body of Adam and also his bride. The
Church is the nearest and the most beloved object to
His loving heart. "He loved the Church and gave
Himself for it; that He might sanctify and cleanse it
with the washing of the water by the word, that He
might present to Himself a glorious church not having
spot, or wrinkle, or any such thing; but that it should
be holy and without blemish" (Eph. v: 25-27). She

is the pearl of great price for which He sold all He had. The Church is this bride of Christ, and even before the marriage the Spirit of God in anticipation addressed her as such. "For I have espoused you to one husband, that I may present you as a chaste virgin to Christ" (2 Cor. xi: 2). And when the Holy Spirit gives the blessed exhortation to the Christian family and indicates its deeper meaning, that the Christian family is typical of Christ and the Church, He adds "I speak concerning Christ and the Church." For we are members of His body, of His flesh and of His bones. The church is now presented in glory to Himself; this is before us in this passage. She comes into view as the Lamb's wife. It is very significant that the twenty-four Elders are no longer mentioned after this. As we saw the twenty-four Elders are typical of all the redeemed, the Saints of both Testaments. But here a division takes place. The bride, the church takes her exalted position along side of Himself and the Old Testament Saints are there as the friends of the Bridegroom (John iii: 29). But they do not belong to the Church and do not compose the bride of Christ.

But how has she made herself ready? And what does it mean "And to her was granted that she should be arrayed in fine linen, clean and white for the linen is the righteousness of the Saints"? The Grace of God has supplied the robe and the precious blood is her title to glory. In this respect she was ready. But the words here refer us to the judgment seat of Christ, that award seat before which we must appear. Then the hidden things are brought to light and the wood and the hay and stubble is burned (1 Cor. iii: 12-15).

Then "every man shall have praise of God" (1 Cor. iv: 5) and what Grace accomplished in each one and through each will be manifested. And the clean white linen "is the righteousness of the Saints." The word "righteousness" is in the plural. It means more than the righteousness which we are in Christ or the faith in Him, which is counted for righteousness (Rom. iv: 3). It includes all the blessed results in life and service produced by the Holy Spirit, the practical righteousness of the Saints. And yet even these need the washing in that precious blood without which all is unclean and unholy. And so it is Grace after all as indicated by the word "given."*—"it was given to her to be clothed in fine linen, bright and pure." He Himself has made her ready and removed every spot, every wrinkle and every blemish. God grant that we His people may daily meditate on this coming glorious event, the marriage of the Lamb, and walk worthy of such a Lord and such a calling. Once more John is commissioned to write. "Write, Blessed are they which are bidden to the marriage supper of the Lamb." And who can estimate the blessedness of being in His ever blessed Presence, at His table, at the marriage supper of the Lamb! And to this feast sinners are called by the Gospel throughout this age, and they who accept the gracious invitation, and become His, can look forward with holy anticipation to the coming marriage and the marriage supper, the feast of joy and gladness. And to this is added the very seal of God. "These are the true words of

---

* Revised Version.

God." What assurance this gives to our souls! Because these are the very words of God, all will come to pass as promised here. It does not matter if our years come and go, the ultimate accomplishment will surely come. And John was overwhelmed and fell at the feet of the angel to worship him. Beautiful it is how the angel takes the place as a servant, a fellow-servant of those that have the testimony of Jesus. The testimony of Jesus is the spirit of Prophecy. And the testimony of Jesus bears witness to His resurrection, His presence in glory, and His coming again, and all the blessed things connected with that day, so fully revealed in God's Word. Thus the testimony of Jesus is the spirit of Prophecy. All Prophecy concerns the Lord Jesus Christ and all intelligent, scriptural proclamation of the coming events are a testimony concerning Himself.

2. Heaven Opened. The Coming of the King. Verses 11-16. And now we reach the great event so often mentioned in the Old Testament, the event for which this world is waiting, the visible manifestation of Him, whom the heavens received, who returns to judge the earth, to receive the promised Kingdom and rule over the earth for a thousand years. We have reached the great climax in the Revelation. In the beginning of the book we read the announcement "Behold, He cometh with clouds and every eye shall see Him," and now this long predicted and long expected event takes place. To quote the predictions in the Old Testament prophetic Word which speak of the Coming of the King and His rule would fill many pages. Without quoting the words we give a number of passages which every student of Revelation should read and become familiar with, for they shed their light upon this chapter. Psalm ii; xlv; xlvi; xlvii; l: 1-6; lxviii; cx; Isaiah xi; xxiv: 19-23; xxv; xxvi: 20-21; lxiii: 1-6; lxv: 5-16. Daniel ii: 44-45; vii: 9-14; Joel iii; Habak. iii; Zech. xiv. These are but a few of many more which could be added. His own words are to be fulfilled. "Immediately after the tribulation of those days shall the sun be darkened, and the moon shall not give her light, and the stars shall fall from heaven, and the powers of the heaven shall be shaken. And then shall appear the sign of the Son of Man in heaven, and then shall the tribes of the earth mourn, and they shall see the Son of Man coming on the clouds of heaven with power and great glory" (Matt. xxiv: 29-30). The angel's message which was given when He ascended into glory is now to be accomplished. "This same Jesus, which is taken up from you into heaven, shall so come in like manner as ye have seen Him go into heaven" (Acts i: 11). The words of the Spirit of God addressed to the Thessalonians are also coming to pass. "The Lord Jesus shall be revealed from heaven with His mighty angels, in flaming fire taking vengeance on them that know not God, and that obey not the Gospel of our Lord Jesus Christ, who shall perish with everlasting destruction from the presence of the Lord, and from the glory of His power; when He shall come to be glorified in His Saints and marvelled at in all them that believed—in that day" (2 Thess. i: 7-10).

Impressive words—"And I saw heaven opened." Heaven was opened unto Him when He came out of

Jordan at His baptism. While His baptism foreshadowed His death in the sinner's place, His resurrection and ascension are foreshadowed in coming out
of the waters and the open heaven. In heaven at
the right hand of God He has been ever since, unseen
by human eyes. At last the time has come when
God is to make His enemies as the footstool of His
feet. Heaven is opened so that He might be revealed
in His glorious majesty. And out of the opened
heavens He comes forth. "Gird thy sword upon thy
thigh, O most mighty, with thy glory and majesty.
And in thy majesty ride prosperously, because of truth
and meekness; and thy right hand shall teach thee
terrible things. Thine arrows are sharp in the heart
of the King's enemies, whereby the people fall under
thee" (Ps. xlv: 3-5). Thus the inspired Psalmist fore-
saw long ago the great event. He comes as the mighty
Victor to judge in righteousness and to make war.
"And behold a white horse; and He that sat thereon
was called Faithful and True and in righteousness
He doth judge and make war." The white horse is
symbolical of victorious warfare and glorious conquest. When, seven years before the first seal had
been opened (vi: 1), a rider appeared upon a white
horse achieving great conquest. It was the false
king who was seen then in vision. He is as the Beast
on earth with the King and their armies to make
war with the coming King who comes out of the opened
heaven. Glorious sight! He is coming to conquer
and to claim His inheritance. The appointed day has
come in which God "will judge the world in righteousness by that man, whom He hath ordained;

whereof He has given assurance unto all men in that
He hath raised Him from the dead" (Acts xvii: 31).
Upon His head are many diadems. The Saints wear
crowns, but He to whom belongs all power in heaven
and on earth wears many diadems, encircling His head
in dazzling splendour. We look back to see Him
wearing a crown of thorns, the emblems of the curse.
What a scene it was when Pilate led Him forth with
His face marred and dishonored and the cruel thorns
piercing His blessed brow! And now God has crowned
Him with supreme authority and He appears in Glory
to exercise His rights over the earth. It will be God's
vindication of His ever blessed Son. His Person and
His Work has been denied and rejected. Boastingly
a certain leader of the so-called "new theology"*
preached not long ago on "the vanishing Christ." He
meant by it the denial of the doctrine of Christ, His
essential Deity, the virgin birth, His sacrificial death
and His physical resurrection. Thus apostate Christendom rejects His Person, and the time comes during the great apostasy when they think He is a van-
ished Christ. But when He comes as the vanquishing
Christ, then His Person will be fully vindicated by
that glorious event.

"And He had a name written, that no man knew but
Himself." And again it is written "His Name is
called the Word of God." And on His vesture and on
His thigh there is a name written "King of kings and
Lord of lords." The unknown Name is the name of
His essential Deity. No human name can express

---

*It is not a new theology, for it is the Devil's lie as old
as Eden; nor is it theology, but only foolish ramblings.

what He is in Himself. "No man knoweth the Son but the Father." His name "the Word of God" refers us to the Gospel of John. As the Word He is the express image of God, that is He makes God visible. He is the expression of God in His character, His thoughts and counsels. And the third name mentioned "King of kings and Lord of lords" expresses what He is in relation to the earth.

"And he was clothed with a vesture dipped in blood"—"And out of His mouth goeth a sharp sword, that with it He should smite the nations, and He shall rule them with a rod of iron, and He treadeth the winepress of the fierceness and wrath of Almighty God." The blood dipped vesture has nothing to do with His work on the cross. He is described in Isaiah lxiii: 1-4 as the One who has the day of vengeance in His heart, and this passage in Isaiah is here being fulfilled. The two edged sword refers us to Isaiah xi: 4. "He shall smite the earth with the rod of His mouth and with the breath of His lips shall He slay the wicked." See also 2 Thess. ii: 8. The sentence "He shall rule them (the nations) with a rod of iron" is quoted from the Second Psalm. In that Psalm we read that God saith to Him "Ask of Me and I will give thee the nations for thine inheritance and the uttermost parts of the earth for Thy possession." And He asked God after His own had been gathered home, and the answer is here seen. He comes to rule* the nations and to execute the wrath of Almighty God upon His enemies. But He is not alone. The armies of heaven follow the great King. They are like Him

---

* Literal "shepherd."

upon white horses and are clothed in fine linen, **white** and clean. These armies are not angels. It is true angels will be with Him as He comes, for it is written then He shall be revealed with His holy angels. Angels will be the reapers in the judgment (Matt. xiii: 41) when the age ends and they will be used in the re-gathering of Israel. (Matt. xxiv: 31). But the armies here are not angels. They are the glorified Saints; the fine linen, white and clean identifies them fully. In faith and blessed assurance, you dear reader and the writer can say, we shall be in that company with Himself as leader. The Son brings His many sons unto glory (Heb. ii: 10). What a sight that will be for the earth-dwellers! Each in that company bears His own image; each reflects His own Glory. Then He will be marvelled at in them that had believed (2 Thess. i: 10). It is the fulfillment of what St. Paul wrote to the Colossians: "When Christ, who is our life shall appear, then shall ye also appear with Him in Glory" (Col. iii: 4). The first Prophet mentioned in the Bible, Enoch, had predicted this event for he prophesied "Behold the Lord cometh with ten thousands of His Saints to execute judgment" (Jude, verse 14). Zechariah saw it in connection with the gathering of the armies against Jerusalem, when the Lord will fight against those nations. He announced "the Lord my God shall come and all the Saints with Thee" (Zech. xiv: 5). And the Saints who come with Him share His triumph, His glory, and are partakers in the judgment and in the reign which follows. "Know ye not that the Saints shall judge the world?" (1 Cor. vi: 2.) Oh! beloved readers what a future is ours!

To be with Him forever and like Him in glory never-ending! And the Saints are seen in this new aspect corresponding to what He is and what He does. We shall then be one with Him in the fullest sense of the word.

3. *The Battle of Armageddon and the Execution of Wrath. Verses 17-21.* And what a sublime vision comes next! An angel is beheld by the seer standing in the sun, and with a loud voice he summons the birds that fly in mid-heaven to gather themselves to the great supper of God* to eat the flesh of the slain. The birds of prey are summoned in anticipation of the battle of Armageddon which is then imminent. What a contrast this great supper here is with another great supper of which we read in the Gospel of Luke! (Chapter xiv: 15-24). One had said to the Lord "Blessed is he that shall eat bread in the Kingdom of God." Then He spoke of a great supper which one had made, inviting the guests "Come! for all things are now ready." It is the supper of love and grace which God, at the infinite cost-price, the price which His Son paid on the cross, provided for lost sinners. For almost two thousand years the invitation has gone out and uncountable multitudes have come and have partaken of the riches of His Grace. But the invitation has also been rejected. Yea, as the age draws to its close the rejection of the Gospel, of the cross of Christ, the precious blood, which alone can open heaven and close forever the gates of hell, becomes more universal and more pronounced. Not

---

* The authorized version has it "the supper of the great God" which is incorrect; it is "the great supper of God."

alone are the great masses in Christendom rejecting
the Gospel of Grace wilfully, but they are also accept-
ing Satan's lies and delusions, such as "salvation by
characters," and the anti-christian cults like "Christian
Science"—"Theosophy" and the "new theology." As
long as the Lord leaves His Church on earth the sound
of the true Gospel can never die out. It will be heard
as long as God's true people, who know the Gospel and
love it, are on earth. But after the rapture of the
Church it will be different. Then all who received not
the love of the truth but had pleasure in unrighteous-
ness, will be hardened; the strong delusion which
comes into the world through Satan and his demons
will be accepted by them. (2 Thess. ii: 10-12). We
have seen this class in previous chapters, they are
called, "the dwellers on the earth." They are the
apostates who reject the Gospel, refuse to come to the
great supper of God's love, and even the severest judgments of God did not lead them to repentance. Instead
of crying "God be merciful to me, a sinner" they blas-
phemed (ix: 20-21). And now the hour of judgment
has come. Another supper is spread. An angel,
standing in the sun, the place of supreme authority,
gives the invitation to the birds of prey to be ready
for the feast which a holy and righteous God will have
for them. The day of wrath has come. The slain of
the Lord shall be many (Isaiah lxvi: 16).

And down on earth there is the greatest gathering
of armies the world has ever seen. The Beast, the
head of the revived Roman empire, is the commander-
in-chief. The kings of the earth are with him. Vast
army camps on all sides. The great valley on the

plains of Esdrælon is filled with soldiers. The hills and mountains swarm with armed men. Satan's power has gathered and blinded this vast multitude to the utmost. The unclean spirits, the demons working miracles, have brought them together to the battle of that day. And the hordes from the North, under the Prince of Rosh are coming later. These vast multitudes from the North and beyond Euphrates are described in Ezekiel xxxviii-xxxix. And in that Old Testament prophecy we find a statement which reminds us of the great supper of God here in Revelation. "Speak unto every feathered fowl, and to every beast of the field, assemble yourselves and come; gather yourselves on every side to my sacrifice that I do sacrifice for you, even a great sacrifice upon the mountains of Israel, that ye may eat flesh, and drink blood" (Ezek. xxxix: 17). "Thus shall ye be filled at my table with horses and chariots, with mighty men, and with all men of war, saith the Lord God" (verse 20).

Zechariah xiv: 2 is now being fulfilled. While the vast armies are covering valleys and hills, the objective will be Jerusalem. All nations are gathered against her. "For I will gather all nations against Jerusalem to battle; and the city shall be taken, and the houses rifled, and the women ravished; and half of the city shall go forth into captivity, and the residue of the people shall not be cut off from the city." Jerusalem's distress is the greatest of her history. And the faithful remnant looks up for the promised deliverance. The Beast, the Emperor of the empire and the second Beast, the Anti-christ, called also the false Prophet, act together in this final drama. They are seen together in verse 20.

And now as these armies are massed together the great battle of Armageddon takes place. They are ready to make war against Him, who comes through heaven's portals. Satan has been the usurper for almost 6,000 years. As god of this age he controlled the kingdoms of this earth; he held them in his grasp. He whose right it is, who bought the earth with His blood is about to claim the earth and to receive the kingdom. And Satan makes a great attempt to dispute His authority. And military Christendom, the Gentile nations who even now as we write murder each other for the sake of having dominion, are Satan's instruments in this. He goads them on with the supremest hatred to fight the King of kings, and so to speak, keep Him back from taking possession of the kingdoms of this world. Armageddon means "the mount of slaughter." It is the great plain of Esdraelon which has been described as follows:

"It is called, by way of eminence, 'the great plain in Scripture, and elsewhere, 'the great plain,' or 'field of Esdraelon,' 'the field of Megiddo,' the 'Galilean plain,' which we found one vast meadow covered with the richest pasture. It has been a chosen place for encampment in every contest from the days of Nabuchonodosor, king of Assyria, to the disastrous march of Napoleon Bonaparte into Syria. Jews, Gentiles, Saracens, Christian Crusaders, and anti-Christian Frenchmen, Egyptians, Persians, Druses, Turks and Arabs, warriors of every nation that is under heaven, have pitched their tents on the plain of Esdraelon, and have beheld the banners of their nations wet with the dew of Tabor and Hermon."

See also Joel iii: 2, 9-12. And then heaven has opened. The prayers of the Jewish remnant are answered. Triumphantly they will say as they see the heavenly glory, the returning Shekinah, "Lo, this is our God; we have waited for Him, and He will save us; this is the Lord; we have waited for Him; we will be glad and rejoice in His salvation" (Is. xxv: 9). "Then shall the Lord go forth, and fight against those nations." (Zech. xiv: 2). The battle does not consume much time. Sennacherib's army was suddenly smitten and they all perished, and here are armies in comparison with which Sennacherib's forces were insignificant. One mighty blow from above, one flash of glory and all their strength and power is gone. The stone has fallen (Dan. ii). With one blow the dominion and misrule of the Gentiles is at an end. The Kings of the present day might profitably listen to Nebuchadnezzar's letter in Daniel iv. He began at the times of the Gentiles, and has left this letter to be read by his successors. The words our Lord spoke while on earth "on whom this stone falls it shall grind him to powder" have been fulfilled (Matt. xxi: 44). Such is the awful fate which "Christian civilization (?)" and "Kultur (!)" and a Christ-less Christendom is rapidly approaching. Oh! that the kings and rulers would hear His word. "Be wise now therefore, O ye kings; be instructed ye judges of the earth. Serve the Lord with fear, and rejoice with trembling. Kiss the Son, lest He be angry and ye perish in the way—yet a little and His wrath will be kindled" (Ps. ii: 9-12). But they will not hear. They cast away His Word and ere long the times of the Gentiles will end forever in this indescribable catastrophe. And while the armies perish as to the body and God's wrath sweeps the earth clean of the mass of apostates, taking vengeance on them that know not God and that obey not the Gospel, the Beast (the head of the empire) and the false Prophet (the second Beast of chapter xiii), that is the false Messiah, the Anti-christ, are cast alive into a lake of fire burning with brimstone.* They were not annihilated, for a thousand years later we still find them there (xx: 10); and still they are in existence and will ever be as individuals in that place of eternal punishment. And those that were slain as to the body will be raised after the millennium and also share the place with the two, whom they followed and worshipped.

Chapter XX. *4. The Binding of Satan. Verses 1-3.* And now Satan, who was cast out of heaven three and one-half years before the visible and glorious coming of the Lord, and who has been on earth in person, though not beheld by human eyes, is now seized to be put into his prison for a thousand years. And the demons, who were liberated by Satan (chapter ix) are likewise shut up into the bottomless pit, though this is not mentioned because it is self-evident. The terms "key" and "great chain" are of course

---

* The King of the North, the great invader (the Assyrian of the end-time) will also be cast into the lake of fire. See Isaiah xxx, 33.

figurative. He is mentioned in all his infamous titles. He is called dragon on account of his horrible cruelty and vileness, the old serpent on account of his maliciousness, guile and deception; he is the devil; the archtempter of man, and Satan because he is the accuser of the brethren, the one who opposed Christ and His people. He is now dethroned as the god of this age, completely stripped of his power and his dethronement means the complete enthronement of our Lord Jesus Christ. And here is the important statement that this being, the once glorious Lucifer, the Son of the morning and light-bearer, who fell through pride, has been the deceiver of the nations. It would take pages to describe his deceptions and his lies. Never before has he been so successful as now, blinding the eyes of them that believe not. Idolatry and all the perversions of the Truth of God are his work. He is the author and supporter of every cult which denies Christ. He is the real parent of Higher criticism, Mormonism, Russellism, Christian Science, Spiritism, Theosophy, Romanism, and all other isms which deny the Truth of God. No blessing can be expected, no millennium of this earth, till he is bound and thus completely restrained from deceiving the nations. And this is done. What a happy day it will be when he is shut up. Interesting and helpful in connection with these opening verses of our chapter are the words we find in Isaiah's little apocalypse (Is. xxiv-xxvii). "And it shall come to pass in that day (the day of the Lord's glorious manifestation) that the Lord shall punish the host of the high ones on high, and the kings of the earth upon the earth. And they shall be gathered together as prisoners are gathered in the pit, and shall be shut up in the prison, and after many days shall they be visited" (Is. xxiv : 21-22).

5. *The Reign of Christ and His Saints for a Thousand Years. Verses 4-6.* Thrones are seen next by the Seer. "And I saw thrones, and they sat upon them and judgment was given unto them." Daniel also saw thrones in connection with the judgment of the Beast, but nothing is said of those occupying the thrones in Daniel's vision. Here we have the complete revelation, and several times the blessed statement is made that Christ and His Saints shall reign with Him for a thousand years. The new age in which all things are put in subjection of His feet, the personal reign of Christ, in which all His redeemed people have a share, begins. It will last a thousand years. Six times we read of the thousand years in this chapter. Because this coming age will last a thousand years it has been called by the Latin word "millennium," not a few have made the astonishing declaration that such a period of time during which Christ and His Saints reign over the earth has but little foundation in the Scripture. It is quite true that the only place in which the duration of such an age is given is this great final Book of Revelation. And that should be sufficient for any Christian to believe in such an age of a thousand years. However, this age of unspeakable blessing and glory for this earth is revealed throughout the entire Bible. The Old Testament contains hundreds of unfulfilled promises of blessing for Israel, the nations of the earth and even for all creation, which have never seen even a partial fulfillment.

Isaiah is full of such promises. In the New Testament there are also passages which clearly teach and point to such an age of glory for this earth. Read Matt. xix: 28; Acts iii: 19-21; Romans viii: 19-23; Eph. 1: 10; Col. i: 20; Phil. ii: 9-11. What awful disheartening pessimism it would be if we had to believe, that the terrible conditions prevailing on the earth now, conditions which have steadily become worse, were to continue and that man's work is to remedy them and produce something better. This earth has a bright and glorious future. Nations will some day no longer turn, as they do now their plowshares into swords, but change their swords into plowshares. Righteousness and peace will surely kiss each other and creation's curse and travail pains will end. Mercy and truth meet together.

But when? Never as long as the great unfoldings of this book, which we have briefly followed, have not come to pass. There can be no better day for the earth as long as He is absent and not on the throne, which belongs to Him. But when He comes, when He has appeared in glory and in majesty, then the earth will find her rest and groaning creation will be delivered. As we do not write on the great blessings and glories to come when He comes, we must refrain from following these things. Here in our book the revelation is given that Christ shall reign for a thousand years and His Saints shall reign with Him. Let us notice briefly the different classes mentioned who are associated with Christ in His personal reign. The entire company of the redeemed, as we saw them under the symbolical figure of the twenty-four Elders, occupying thrones and wearing crowns, are undoubtedly meant by the first statement "they sat upon them and judgment was given unto them." They judge with Him. This is the raptured company whom we saw first in glory in chapters iv and v; and we, dear fellow-believer, belong to this company. Then follow the martyrs, which we saw under the fifth seal (vi: 9-11) "And I saw the souls of them that had been beheaded on account of the testimony of Jesus and for the Word of God." Then we have a third company. "And I saw those who had not worshipped the Beast, nor his image, and had not received his mark on their forehead, or in their hands." These are the other martyrs who were slain during the great tribulation, when the Beast set up the image and demanded its worship (xiii). They lived and reigned with Christ a thousand years. The first resurrection is passed and all who have part in it reign with Christ, are priests of God and of Christ and shall reign with Him a thousand years. Oh! wonderful grace which has saved us! Grace which has saved us in Christ and through His ever precious blood delivered us from eternal perdition! Grace which saved us from Satan's power, from sin and all its curse! Grace which has lifted into such heights of Glory and has made us the sons of God and the joint-heirs of the Lord Jesus Christ! And how little after all we enter into all these things, which ought to be our daily joy and delight. How little we know of the power of the coming glory of being with Christ and reigning with Him! How we do cling to the passing things of a fast passing age. May the Holy Spirit bless us all dear readers as we look forward into the coming glory of sharing the glorious inheritance of our Saviour Lord and may our lives tell out the wonderful story that we are the joint-heirs of Christ.

And even if we were now to enlarge upon the reign of Christ, the throne of Christ, the dominion of Christ, the glory of Christ, the righteous judgments and government of the King, it would be but with a feeble pen and with a stammering tongue. Not the half can be told. But this we know we shall be with Him and enjoy with Him His glorious reign and inheritance. The rest of the dead mentioned in the fifth verse are the wicked dead; we shall hear more of them at the close of this chapter.

NINTH DIVISION: AFTER THE THOUSAND YEARS. THE VISION OF THE NEW JERUSALEM.

Chapters XX: 7-XXII: 5

The Millennium, the thousand years' reign of Christ with His Saints, will be earth's jubilee. From certain sides, especially the Seventh Day Adventists, the statement is made in our days that the world is soon going to end, that God will destroy the earth by fire and thus end all. This is an unscriptural assertion. If it were true and the world would come to an end this year, or next year, the last word would belong to Satan, and God would confess Himself defeated. The blessed redemption work of our Lord would then likewise be proven insufficient to put things back into the condition before sin entered the world. God cannot permit the destruction of the earth in the condition in which it is now. And as already stated the entire Bible bears witness to it that there will come a better day for this earth before the predicted destruction by fire comes. And that promised age of blessing and glory comes when the King, our Lord, has come and reigns in righteousness with His Saints over the earth. "For He *must* reign till He hath put all enemies under His feet. The last enemy that shall be destroyed is death. For he hath put all things under His feet. But when He saith, All things are put under Him, it is manifest that He is excepted, which did put all things under Him" (1 Cor. xv: 25-27). In that age which begins, as we have seen, with His visible manifestation, the unfulfilled predictions of the Old Testament will find their literal and most blessed fulfillment. "In His days shall the righteous flourish; and abundance of peace, so long as the moon endureth. He shall have dominion also from sea to sea and from the river unto the ends of the earth" (Ps. lxxii: 7-8). "And He shall judge among the nations, and shall rebuke many people, and they shall beat their swords into plowshares and their spears into pruning hooks, nation shall not lift sword up against nation neither shall they learn war any more" (Isaiah ii: 4). "The wolf and the lamb shall feed together, and the lion shall eat straw like the bullock, and dust shall be the serpent's meat; they shall not hurt or destroy in all my holy mountain, saith the Lord" (Isaiah lxv: 25). And many other prophecies could be added which will then find a literal accomplishment. Long ago Jehovah had said "But as truly as I live all the earth shall be filled with the glory of the Lord" (Numb. xiv:21). And this utterance of an Almighty Lord will find its fulfillment in the day when He reigns. "For the earth shall be filled with the knowledge of the glory of the Lord, as the waters cover the sea" (Hab. ii:14). "The whole earth is full of His glory" (Isaiah vi:3). The earth will be full of His glory and there will be an increase and a blessing which no pen can describe.

But this great and glorious future of the earth is not a permanent state. If man had thought this out and invented such a future for this earth, man might have added, that in this blessed condition the earth would remain forever. But no human mind could think out all this; what follows now shows us that we have here revelation.

Chapter XX. *1. Satan Loosed. The Last Revolt. Verses 7-9.* Satan who was put into the abyss a thousand years before, is now loosed out of his prison. God permits him to come forth once more. Who could have ever thought of such a thing! The arch-enemy who had done his vile and wicked work among the human race for a thousand years, put at last into the place of perfect restraint, and now loosed once more to continue, for a brief season, his work! And he finds nations ready for his deception, not a few, but a number "as the sand of the sea." God permits Satan to come out of his prison, so that the absolute corruption of man might be demonstrated. Man has been tried and tested under every possible condition. He has failed in every age. He failed under the law and he failed even more in the grace-dispensation, and now under the most glorious conditions, during the millennium, when the Lord Himself is known in all the earth and reigns in righteousness, when want and nearly all the sorrows of a ruined creation are banished, when there is peace on earth, man also fails and does not fully respond to a gracious Lord. But here is a difficulty which many have. Many a sincere post-Millennialist, who has studied the pre-millennial coming of our Lord, has asked this question, "If the whole world is converted during the millennium, how is it then that Satan finds nations ready to side with him after the thousand year reign of Christ and then leads them on to destruction?" The difficulty is far from being as great as it is generally made. In fact it is easily explained. As far as Israel is concerned, the all Israel living, when He comes, the trusting remnant of Israel, they will constitute the blessed nation in possession of all her promised blessings. They are not mentioned as siding with Satan. No more backsliding for that nation. Isaiah lix: 20-21 vouches for this. "And the Redeemer shall come to Zion (His second coming), and unto them that turn from transgression in Jacob, saith the Lord. As for me, this is my covenant with them, saith the Lord. My Spirit that is upon thee, and my words which I have put in thy mouth, shall not depart out of thy mouth, nor out of the mouth of thy seed, nor out of the mouth of thy seed's seed, saith the Lord, from henceforth and forever." "Neither will I hide my face any more from them for I have poured out my Spirit upon the house of Israel, saith the Lord God" (Ezek. xxxix: 29).

And the Gentile nations in the beginning of the millennium will also be converted. However the human conditions of the earth will continue. The nations are not in a glorified state. Marriage will continue. Children will be born during the millennium. Indeed the earth will be populated as never before. Billions of human beings can be sustained upon our planet and they will come into existence by natural generation during the golden age of glory. Wars will be unknown. No longer will the flower of manhood be cruelly murdered by human passion in that legalized horrible thing called war. Earthquakes will no longer sweep thousands upon thousands into an untimely grave, nor can famines and pestilences claim their millions. Nor will there be the great infant mortality. Physical death will no longer be the universal rule, but rather an exception (See Isaiah lxv:20). Now every child born during the millennium of the converted nations comes into the world the same as the children in the present age. It is still true, conceived and born in sin. And it is equally true, they must be born again. And as many children of pious, godly parents in this age are Gospel hardened and live on in sin, though they hear the Gospel and see its power, so in the millennium, an enormous multitude will see the glory, live under the best and most glorious conditions the earth has seen since the fall of man, and yet they will be Glory hardened and only submit to the righteousness of that age and yield obedience through fear, for disobedience to the governing laws of the kingdom on earth, will mean sudden and certain judgment. It is not the obedience produced by a believing, trusting heart, but only a feigned obedience. Three prophetic Psalms which speak of these millennial conditions make this clear, if we consider the marginal reading. "As soon as they hear of Me, they shall obey Me, the strangers shall yield feigned obedience unto Me" (Ps. xviii : 44). "Say unto God, How terrible art Thou in Thy works! Through the greatness of Thy power shall Thine enemies yield feigned obedience unto Thee" (Ps. lxvi : 3). "The haters of the Lord yield feigned obedience unto Him, *but* their time might have endured forever" (lxxxi : 15). Study these Psalms in their millennial bearing. Thus many nations submit while sin is in their heart and in their blindness they long and hope for the day when they may cast off the restraint.* And that day comes when Satan is loosed

---

*In the Millennium, the heavenly is displayed in connection with the earthly. The glory of God is manifested, so that the earth is filled with the knowledge of it as the waters cover the sea. Righteousness rules, and evil is afraid to lift its head. The curse is taken from the ground, which responds with wondrous fruitfulness. Amid all this, the spiritual condition is by no means in correspondence with the outward blessing. Even the manifest connections of righteousness and prosperity cannot avail to make men love righteousness; nor the goodness of God, though evidenced on every side, to bring men to repentance. At the "four corners of the earth," retreating as far as possible, from the central glory, there are still those who represent Israel's old antagonists, and thus are called by their names "Gog and Magog." Nor are they remnants, but masses of populations brought together by sympathetic hatred of God and His people—crowding alike out of light into the darkness: a last and terrible answer to the question, "Lord, what is man?" —F. W. G.

out of his prison to deceive these nations which are in the four quarters of the earth. Nor must we overlook the fact that before all this happened, throughout the millennium, the nations were warned of the possibility and the consequences of such a revolt. As already quoted in Isaiah lxv: 25 we read that while the curse is removed from animal creation, the serpent alone remains in the place where the curse has placed that creature. "And dust shall be the serpent's meat." The serpent continues crawling in the dust, a warning to the nations that the age of glory and blessing will end in a manifestation of Satan. And there is still another warning voice during the thousand year reign of Christ. "And it shall come to pass, that from one new moon to another, and from one sabbath unto another, shall all flesh come to worship before Me, saith the Lord. And they shall go forth and look upon the carcases of the men that have transgressed against Me; for their worm shall not die, neither shall their fire be quenched, and they shall be an abhorring unto all flesh" (Is. lxvi: 23-24). Here we read that during the millennium the nations will go up to Jerusalem to worship there. And after they have done so and beheld the visible glory of the Lord, which will be seen in and above the city, they will be led out to look upon a most awful scene. There at one side of Jerusalem is a deep valley. In looking down they behold the carcases of the men who transgressed against the Lord. Their bodies are seen; a never dying worm gnaws there and an unquenchable fire burns. An awful picture of another place, where the worm does not die and the fire is not quenched.

It is a solemn warning to these nations that the story of sin and apostasy is not yet completed.

Gog and Magog here must not be identified with Gog and Magog of Ezekiel xxxviii and xxxix. The invasion of Israel's land described by Ezekiel took place before the millennium, it is pre-millennial. Gog and Magog here must not be taken in a literal meaning, it is used metaphorically. The invasion before the millennium is the prototype of this final revolt. Utterly blinded, as these multitudes must be, they follow willingly Satan's leadership. Gathering from the four corners of the earth they compass the camp of the Saints and the beloved city. The beloved city is Jerusalem. The "camp of the Saints" may mean the heavenly Saints. The redeemed are above the earth in the new Jerusalem, and yet they have also access to the earth and are with the King in the government of the earth. Nothing is said about the camp of the Saints and the beloved city. They know the outcome. God permits the invading hosts with Satan at the head to compass them. But suddenly God acts. A swift and awful judgment overtakes them. Solemnly brief is the announcement "fire came down from God out of heaven and devoured them." Not a wicked one is left; the earth is completely purged of evil-doers.

2. The Devil's Eternal Doom. Verse 10. It was the final attempt of the dethroned usurper to regain his lost dominion. For thousands of years, in the all-wise purposes of God, he was permitted to be the prince of the power of the air and the god of this age. We have followed his history in this book and seen how he was cast out of heaven upon the earth where he caused the great tribulation. Then we beheld him stripped of all his power. The kingdoms of the world became the kingdom of Christ and the old serpent was cast into the abyss where he remained a thousand years. Loosed for a little season he tried once more to become earth's master. And fire out of heaven devoured the nations who had revolted. The devil receives his final doom. He is cast into the lake of fire and brimstone. He goes to a fixed place, a locality where unspeakable and eternal torment is his portion. This place is prepared for the devil and his angels (Matt. xxv:41). And all the wicked will share that place. And he finds others there. The first beings who were cast into this final abode were the Beast (the emperor of the Roman empire, the little horn of Dan. vii), and the false prophet (the personal Anti-christ, the second Beast of chapter xiii). They were put there a thousand years before and as they are there as persons it shows they were not annihilated. Annihilation is an unscriptural and evil doctrine. And they shall be tormented day and night for ever and ever—for the ages of ages—never ending—for all eternity. What a solemn truth this is! Yet men meddle with it and deny future, conscious and eternal punishment. Besides these three persons, the nations who were judged and condemned in the beginning of the millennium, when the Son of Man sat upon the throne of His glory (Matt. xxv:31) are also in the Lake of Fire.

"There is an awful fitness in the sovereign arrangement of the holy God, that the devil, and those who, by persistence in sin, had made themselves more and

more like him, should spend their eternity together—
and that eternity in a place shut out from all that is
good, which they had hated, and in outer darkness,
where there is wailing and gnashing of teeth. And
of this hell-fire, into which those wicked living on
the earth were cast when Christ had judged them, the
language used is, that it was *'prepared* for the devil
and his angels.' But these words seem certainly to
imply that he had not *then* been cast into it."*

3. *The Great White Throne Judgment. Verses 11-
15.* And now we reach the last great judgment scene
of God's holy Word. Much confusion prevails among
Christians about this judgment. There is no such
thing in the Word of God as a universal judgment,
nor is there a universal resurrection. Every human
being which has died will be raised at some time. Our
Lord spoke (John v:28) of two resurrections, a resurrection unto life and a resurrection unto judgment.
The Revelation speaks of the first resurrection. "This
is the first resurrection" (xx:5). And before the
Apostle wrote of a resurrection from among the dead
(Phil. iii:11). The first resurrection was finished
in the beginning of the millennium. "But the rest
of the dead lived not again until the thousand years
were finished." The rest of the dead come now into
view and they are of necessity the wicked dead, who
died in their sins, and whose is the resurrection unto
judgment. Some, like "Pastor" Russell, who echoes
the evil teachings of others, have invented a third
resurrection, a resurrection of the unsaved for a
second chance. In the light of this final Bible book

---

*Lincoln on Revelation.

there is no room whatever for such a resurrection, which would give the lost another opportunity. Nor does the rest of the Bible mention such a third resurrection. And this great judgment is not a universal judgment. It is taught that the entire human race, the living and the dead, will appear before this great white throne. But this is incorrect, for it saith "I saw the dead, small and great, stand before God." No living people are there at all. Again the judgment-scene in Matthew xxv: 31, etc., is spoken of as being the universal judgment and identical with the judgment here in Revelation. But this is another error. In the judgment of Matthew xxv the dead are not there, but living nations are judged in the beginning of the millennium. And these nations are judged on account of the treatment of the Jewish preachers of the Gospel of the Kingdom heralded by them during the last seven years of the age. They did not accept the last offer of mercy and that is why they treated the messengers as they did. Furthermore the throne which the Son of Man occupies in Matthew xxv is upon the earth; the throne in Revelation xx: 11 comes into view after earth and heaven fled away. The church and the Saints of God are not concerned at all in the judgment of Matthew xxv, nor in the great white throne judgment. They are at that time in His own presence glorified. Every Christian should have these things clearly defined and know that for him, as in Christ, there is no more judgment or condemnation (John v: 24; Rom. viii: 1). The judgment seat of Christ before which believers have to appear

(2 Cor. v: 10) does not concern their eternal salvation, but their works and rewards.

Who is the occupant of this great White Throne? Not God the Father, but God the Son. "The Father judgeth no man but hath committed all judgment unto the Son" (John v: 22). The earth and heaven fled from His face. Sin-stained and defiled as they were they flee away from the face of the holy One. The great conflagration of 2 Peter iii: 7-12 takes place. Fire of judgment swept the earth before the millennium, the day of the Lord, began; but the all consuming fire comes after the millennium. Out of that great conflagration there arises a new heaven and a new earth (xxi: 1).

"One could readily imagine that the *present* scene, so marred and wrecked, would at once disappear before the glory and majesty of such an One, but that is not what is seen here. It is the earth and the heaven constituted by the Lord Himself as spheres to display His glory and righteousness, that cannot abide the glory of His face. The millennial scene, both in its higher and lower departments, is at the best an imperfect condition. 'The earth and heaven fled'—not passed out of existence, not annihilated—the next clause carefully guards against any such unscriptural deduction, 'place was not found for them.' It does intimate the complete disappearance of the millennial earth and heaven. Consequent upon the removal of these, new heavens and a new earth fitted, furnished, and constituted for eternity take their place—are made, (Isa. lxvi: 22; 2 Peter iii: 13). Between the passing away of the millennial scene and the introduction of the eternal world, material in both cases—the great white throne is set up. This consideration imparts profound solemnity to the scene before us. For the throne is not set on the earth, nor in relation to its dispensations and times. It is a scene outside human history entirely. We have passed *out* of time and *into* eternity. The judgment therefore of the throne is final and in its very nature eternal. We are in God's eternity. There can be no measures of time nor limitations bounded by the globe, for that by which all is measured and limited has passed away. The judgment is of souls in their individual relation to God and is consequently final and eternal."*

But what about the millions of saved Israelites and Gentiles who are on the millennial earth? Where are they during this great conflagration? What becomes of them? "That they share the eternal blessings and glories in the eternal state is certain. But their abode between the burning of the earth and the calling into existence of the new heaven and the new earth is unrevealed. Speculation on it would be wrong. We should accept the silences of Scripture as much in faith as we accept the promises of God.

And John sees the dead standing before the Throne. Books were opened and another book was opened, the book of life. "And the dead were judged out of the things which were written in the books, according to their works." The books are symbolical; conscience and memory will speak loudly. Twice we read that they are judged according to their works. Upon

---

* W. Scott on Revelation.

Romans v : 12, the marginal reading "in whom (Adam) all have sinned" some have taught that man is held responsible for the sin of Adam and the corrupt nature man has. But that is a mistake. We are not held responsible for having a fallen nature. We are responsible for the outworking of that nature. Therefore the dead are judged "according to their works." And in the "Book of Life" none of their names were written, or they would not have been in that company. "All this would seem to show that, though a millennium has passed since the first resurrection, yet no *righteous* dead can stand among this throng. The suggestion of the "Book of Life" has seemed to many to imply that there are such; but it is not said that there are, and the words "whosoever was not found written in the Book of Life was cast into the lake of fire" may be simply a solemn declaration (now affirmed by the result) that grace is man's only possible escape from the judgment."*

The second resurrection takes place. The sea gives up the dead and death and hades give up the dead. Hades gives up the souls, and Death, used here for the grave, gives up the bodies. Death and Hades were cast into the lake of fire. Both had come into existence because man had sinned, and therefore they are cast into the place, where all belongs which is contrary to the holiness and righteousness of God. And then that solemn word! "And whosoever was not found written in the Book of Life was cast into the lake of fire." It corresponds to that other solemn statement in John iii : 36. "He that believeth on the

---

* Numerical Bible.

Son hath everlasting life; and he that believeth not the Son shall not see life, but the wrath of God abideth upon him." To be written in the "Book of Life" means to have life in Christ. Not our works, not our character, not our religiousness, not our tears, our prayers and our service can put our names in the "Book of Life." Grace alone can do it, and Grace does it as we believe on the Lord Jesus Christ. Reader! is *your* name written there?

The Saints of God are in eternal glory; the wicked dead, the lost are in an eternal lake of fire and suffer conscious, eternal punishment. And how man, blind, presumptuous man, yea even such who know God, rise up against this solemn truth, the eternal punishment of the wicked. They accuse God of injustice, as if the judge of all the earth would not do right. That the suffering of the lost differs is obvious. It is eternal because the evil condition remains unchanged. There is no repentance, no faith, no new birth in hell. As there are different rewards for the faithful service of the saints, so are there different degrees of punishment for the unsaved (Luke xii: 47-48). This is the second death, not blotting out of existence, but endless existence in separation from God. The following helpful summary appeared in "Our Hope."

1. Each individual is in the only possible place for which he is adapted by life and nature—his own place.

2. The varying rewards or penalties have been "worked out" by the individual, and are not indiscriminate.

3. Where there has been no opposing will, as in the case of infants or those irresponsible, then the will of

God is not hindered, and He willeth not the death of any. By the ransom He has found in Christ all such are saved forever.

4. It is due to human will, not divine, that any are lost.

5. Not one protest will then be heard in any part of the universe against the justice of God.

6. All creation will thus be reconciled to, and in harmony at least, in the confession of the righteousness of God.

7. And thus God shall be all in all; the one to whom all submission is accorded, by all, everywhere.*

Chapter XXI. *4. The Eternal State. Verses 1-8.* And now the eternal state comes into view. "And I saw a new heaven and a new earth; for the first heaven and the first earth were passed away and the sea is no more." This is the revelation concerning the final and eternal state of the earth. "Thou hast established the earth and it abideth" (Ps. cxix: 90); "But the earth abideth forever" (Eccl. i: 4). These divine statements are now fulfilled. Many Christians have a very vague conception of the eternal state of the earth and the abode of the redeemed. They think of it as a spiritual state destitute of any locality. But it is not so. The earth and the heaven abide as definite places throughout all eternity. What a marvellous fact this is! In chapter xx: 11 we read that the earth and the heaven fled away and there was found no place. We saw that at that time the great con-

---

* "Our Hope" May, 1915. Notes on Revelation by F. C. J.

flagration of which Peter speaks took place, when "the heaven shall pass away with a great noise and the elements shall be dissolved with fervent heat, the earth also and the works that are therein shall be burned up." (2 Peter iii: 10.) But we read in the same chapter "nevertheless we, according to His promise look for new heavens and a new earth, wherein dwelleth righteousness." (verse 13). During the millennium righteousness reigns upon the earth, but now a state comes for the earth when righteousness shall dwell there. The great burning up meant not an annihilation of the earth and the heavens; God does not annihilate anything, nor does Scripture teach an annihilation of material things and much less the annihilation of human beings, as false teachers claim. The conflagration of the earth and the heaven means their complete purification. We can do nothing better to help in the understanding of this than quoting what another has written on this important and interesting subject.

"Let us look at the question of continuity between the earth that flees away and the earth that succeeds it. At first sight we should surely say, they cannot be identical. The well-known passage in the epistle of Peter would seem to confirm this (2 Peter iii: 10, 12). There we learn that 'the heavens shall pass away with a great noise, and the elements shall melt with fervent heat; the earth also, and the works that are therein, shall be burned up.' And it is repeated, and thus emphasized by repetition, that 'the heavens being on fire shall be dissolved, and the elements shall melt with fervent heat.'

"Yet, as we look more closely, we shall find reason to doubt whether more is meant than the destruction of the earth as the place of human habitation. In the deluge, to which it is compared (verses 5-7), 'the world that then was *perished':* yet its continuity with the present no one doubts. Fire, though the instrument of a more penetrating judgment, yet does not annihilate the material upon which it fastens. The melting even of elements implies rather the reverse, and dissolution is not (in this sense) destruction.

"Yet the heavens and the earth pass away—that is, in the form in which now we know them; or, as the apostle speaks to the Corinthians, 'the *fashion* of this world passes away' (1 Cor. vii:21): and that this is the sense in which we are to understand it, other scriptures come to assure us.

"A 'new' earth does not necessarily mean *another* earth, except as a 'new' man means *another* man— 'new' in the sense of renewed. And even the words here, 'there was no more sea,' naturally suggest another *state* of the earth than now exists. This fact is a significant one: that which is the type of instability and barrenness, and condemns to it so large a portion of the globe, is gone utterly and forever. At the beginning of Genesis we find the whole earth buried under it; emerging on the third day, and the waters given their bounds, which but once afterward they pass. Now they are gone forever, as are the wicked, to whom Isaiah compares it: 'The wicked are like the troubled sea when it cannot rest, whose waters cast up mire and dirt.' This last is the effect of chafing against its bounds, as the 'mind of the flesh' is 'not subject to the law of God, neither indeed can be' (Rom. vii: 7).*

With this we fully agree. The heaven mentioned cannot be the entire heavens; for there is a heaven which cannot be touched by these fires of purification. The heaven is that which surrounds the earth and which was once the peculiar sphere of the great usurper, the prince of the power in the air. And when Peter writes that all this is according to His promise, he had a well-known prophetic statement in Isaiah in mind. "For as the new heaven and the new earth, which I will make, shall remain before me, saith the Lord, so shall your seed and your name remain." (Isaiah lxvi: 22. See also lxv: 17). From this statement we get very definite information that the redeemed Israel established upon the new earth will throughout the eternal state be distinct from the saved nations. They will throughout all eternity bear witness to God's faithfulness as the covenant keeping God. The new heaven and the new earth are therefore the abodes of the redeemed. The new earth, the eternal glory spot of redeemed Israel and the redeemed nations. And the new Jerusalem will come out of heaven to fill the new earth and the new heaven as well. "And I, John, saw the holy city, new Jerusalem, coming down from God out of heaven, prepared as a bride adorned for her husband."

The new Jerusalem, the holy city, comes into view. During the millennium the city of Jerusalem was known as the place of glory for the earth. Numerous Old Testament predictions were fulfilled. See Isaiah

---

* F. W. Grant.

iv: 5-6; liv: 11-14; lx: 11-22. In chapter xx: 9 she is called "the beloved city." But in Revelation iii: 12 we have another Jerusalem mentioned, the same city which John sees coming down out of heaven, the place of the highest glory. It is the church in all her glory; the statement "prepared as a bride adorned for her husband" establishes this beyond controversy. She is called "holy" for all is holy; and a "city" because the Saints are in blessed communion and fellowship there. In the highest glory she had her abode. But now she is being revealed in all her eternal glory and beauty. During the millennial reign this wonderful city was above the earth and from there Christ reigned and His Saints with Him. But here she comes down out of heaven. A thousand years before the marriage of the lamb had taken place (xix: 7-8), and now after a thousand years of unspeakable glory, she is still seen "as a bride adorned for her husband." And yet all these things are given in figurative language. What will be the reality! The masterwork of God is at last fully manifested; what He accomplished through Him, who left the Glory to die on the Cross, is made known. The eternal, never ending riches, purchased by Him who was rich and became poor for our sakes, are beginning to be displayed in all their unfading splendor. Then the Saints of God will learn to know the full meaning of Eph. i: 7, "that in the ages to come He might display the surpassing riches of His grace in kindness towards us through Christ Jesus." "And I heard a loud voice out of heaven, saying, Behold the tabernacle of God is with men, and He will dwell with them, and they shall be His people, and God

Himself shall be with them, and be their God." This is the glorious consummation. It is the goal of a holy, loving God. In Eden He visited man unfallen, walked and talked with Him. Then sin severed this fellowship. He dwelt in the midst of Israel in the holiest of the tabernacle. In this age the church is His habitation by the Spirit, but the blessed consummation in the eternal state will result in God dwelling with His redeemed Creatures. What holy, glorious, never-ending intimacy that will be! It is the time when God is all in all (1 Cor. xv: 28). When that time has come all the former things are passed away. "And God shall wipe away every tear from their eyes, and there shall be no more death, nor sorrow, nor crying, neither shall there be any more pain; for the former things are passed away." Tears, death, sorrow, crying, pain and suffering, these came into existence through sin. And all these things, the effects of sin, are now gone. What relief and what joy! The Saints of God in countless numbers, ever since sin came into the world with all its attending miseries, have looked forward through their tears of sorrow and of pain, to the blessed day when sorrow and sighing should flee away and all mourning be turned into joy. Yea, weeping endureth during the night, the dark night of sin, but joy cometh in the morning. The morning, when the eternal day breaks, will chase all the shadows of the night away. May we learn, in the midst of tears and grief, sorrow and pain, to look forward in holy and blessed anticipation to the day "when God shall wipe away every tear."

Then we hear God's own voice. "And He that sat

on the throne said, Behold I make all things new. And He saith to me, Write: for these words are true and faithful. And He said unto me, It is done. I am Alpha and Omega, the beginning and the end. I will give unto him that is athirst of the fountain of the water of life freely. He that overcomes shall inherit all things; and I will be His God and he shall be my Son." "It is done," tells us that all is now accomplished through the power of God. At the close of the twenty-second Psalm, the Psalm in which the sufferings of Christ and His coming glories are revealed, we find the significant ending, "He hath done it."* When He hung on the cross and was about to bow His blessed head and give His life in death, He said, "It is finished." The great work was done. And that work which was accomplished on the cross is the foundation of everything. Then in chapter xvi: 17, the voice out of the temple from the throne spoke, "It is done." The end of man's day had then come and the day of millennial blessing and glory was ushered in. And here it is for the last time that we find this divine utterance. All is now accomplished; nothing else needs to be done. And it is most blessed to see that the precious Gospel itself is not overlooked. Is the Gospel precious to our hearts? It certainly is to any redeemed one. But we must not forget that the same Gospel is even more precious to God Himself, for in the Gospel His own righteousness has been so wonderfully exalted and His love has been made known. The Gospel is His Gospel and the Gospel of His Son, our Lord Jesus Christ. It is the power of

* Revised Version.

God unto salvation. And so God delights to mention it in this last Book of the Bible a number of times. It was a reminder of the Gospel when we heard in chapter xix, "Blessed are they which are called unto the marriage supper of the Lamb!" And once more in the very end of this book we shall find the Gospel invitation, "And let him that is athirst come. And whosoever will let him come and take the water of life freely." (xxii: 17.) And here it is the Gospel. God, so to speak, in revealing this great consummation in the eternal state, when He will be all in all, sounds forth once more the blessed Gospel promise and assurance. The water of life, He will give freely to all who thirst. And what a consummation of the Gospel, unfathomably deep—"I will be his God, and he shall be my Son!" Perhaps this simple volume may fall into the hands of some who have neglected so great a salvation, who have rejected God's bountiful offer. Then let me speak to you, dear reader. God wants you in His eternal home and glory. Oh! come to Him, who still waits and is ready to give you the water of life freely.

And next comes the eternal state of those who have rejected the Gospel, who lived in their sins and died in their sins, unsaved, unregenerated. "But the fearful, and unbelieving, and abominable, and murderers, and fornicators, and sorcerers, and idolaters, and all liars shall have their part in the lake which burneth with fire and brimstone, which is the second death." God still speaks. How many false teachers are meddling to-day with the solemn Scripture doctrine on the endless punishment of the wicked. Texts of

the Word of God which declare this solemn truth **are**
perverted by them and handled deceitfully. Other
texts which these men declare do not belong in **the**
Bible, they brand as interpolations. But he who
touches these words in this chapter touches the Word
of God Himself, and the teacher who declares that
there is no eternal punishment rejects the very Word
as it comes from God. There is an actual place, the
new heaven and the new earth, for the redeemed; there
is also an actual and everlasting place of punishment
for the last. Eternal is the glory; eternal is the punishment. The human heart, unregenerated, is here un-
covered once more* in the description of those who
find their eternal abode in the lake of fire. And that
lake of fire "burneth"; there is no cessation. It is **a**
fire prepared for the devil and his angels who are
spirits. The fire that causes such intense suffering **to**
the body is the symbol of it.

   *5. The Vision of the Holy City, Jerusalem. Verses
9-27.* We have followed from chapter xix: 1 events
which are chronological. First we heard the Halle-
lujahs in glory, heaven celebrating Babylon's fall.
Then followed the marriage of the Lamb, and **the**
Bride, the glorified church came more fully in view.
We saw heaven opened and the Lord in all his glorious majesty coming forth, attended by the Saints.
The coming of the Lord with His Saints took place.
Then followed the battle of Armageddon, the Beast
and the false prophet were cast into the lake of fire;
the supper of the great God, the day of wrath **had**
come. Satan was cast into the abyss and the **reign of**

---

* See Matt. xv: 19.

Christ with His Saints for a thousand years followed. Without any interruption we saw what happens after the thousand years are complete: Satan loosed for a little season, the final great revolt and its sudden termination by the fire of judgment. Then heaven and earth fled away, the second resurrection and the great white throne judgment. Then we saw the eternal state of the redeemed and the lost.

With the ninth verse we are brought back once more to the millennial state. What was briefly stated in chapter xx: 4-6 is now more fully revealed and we have a description of the Bride, the Lamb's wife in her millennial glory, in relation to Israel and to the nations on the earth. One of the angels which had the seven vials appears on the scene to show something to the Seer. We had a similar scene in chapter xvii: 1-3. There one of these angelic bearers of the vials showed to John, the harlot woman and her judgment; but now he is to see, the Bride, the Lamb's wife. "And he carried me away in the Spirit, and set me on a great, high mountain and showed me the holy City, Jerusalem, coming down out of heaven from God." She is seen coming down out of heaven. This coming down precedes the one mentioned in verses 2-3 by a thousand years. Her coming down does not mean here that she comes actually down upon the earth, to dwell on earth during the millennium. Her coming out of heaven in verses 2-3 is undoubtedly to the new earth. But here she comes down to be over the earth. 1 Thess. iv: 17 may serve as an illustration. When the Lord descends out of heaven with a shout, He does not come down to earth, but He descends to a place above the earth. And so here the Bride, the Lamb's wife, descends out of heaven from God to hover above the earth. This description is symbolical; nor is the city described the Jerusalem on the earth as some have taken it in an ultra-literal sense. The earthly Jerusalem never leaves the earth at all, and the glories of the Jerusalem on the earth during millennial times are fully pictured by the Prophets in the Old Testament; there is no need for an angel to show the beauty and glory spot of the millennial age to John. Isaiah lxii: 2-5 is one of these blessed descriptions of the Jerusalem on the earth. "And the Gentiles shall see thy righteousness, and all kings thy glory, and thou shalt be called by a new name, which the mouth of the Lord shall name. Thou shalt also be a crown of glory in the hand of the Lord and a royal diadem in the hand of thy God. Thou shalt no more be termed Forsaken; neither shall thy land any more be termed Desolate; but thou shalt be called Hephzi-bah (my delight is in her), and thy land Beulah (married); for the Lord delighteth in thee, and thy land shall be married. For as a young man marrieth a virgin, so shall thy sons marry thee, and as the bridegroom rejoiceth over the Bride, so shall thy God rejoice over thee." Such will be Jerusalem's earthly glory and Israel's relation to God throughout the millennium. But here we see the Bride, the Lamb's wife as the holy city Jerusalem descending out of heaven from God. This is the building of God Himself in all its glory, the eternal home of the Saints. "Having the Glory of God." Who is able to understand this one brief sentence? It is more than a reflection of the Glory of God; the very Glory will be her portion. It will be the glorious, though distant vision, for the inhabitants of the earth throughout the millennium. This marvellous city will be seen, resplendent with glory, suspended in the heavens and human eyes will look up to behold the flashes of glory, never ceasing. In Psalm xix we read "the heavens declare the Glory of God and the firmament showeth His handiwork." In beholding the work of His fingers, the moon and the stars, (Psalm viii: 3) we behold now His glory as the omnipotent Creator. But is one of the millennial Psalms, a Psalm which describes the reigning of Jehovah and a rejoicing earth, as well as His judgments, we also read of the heavens and what they will then declare. "The heavens declare His righteousness and all the people see His glory" (Psalm xcvii: 6). This, no doubt, refers to the bright and glorious city, Jerusalem above, as it will be seen by the nations during the coming millennium. "And her light was like unto a stone most precious, even like a Jasper stone, clear as crystal." The Jasper is not transparent. This precious stone mentioned here once more shows the complete identification of the God of Glory with this holy city. (Compare with iv: 3.) "Having a wall great and high, having twelve gates and at the gates twelve angels and names written thereon, which are the names of the twelve tribes of the children of Israel." And this symbolical city, composed not of material stones, but of the living stones, has a great and high wall. A wall, is the means to keep out and to keep in; it denotes separation and security. And of course the city itself is behind the wall. Seven times the number twelve is found in this description. Twelve gates, twelve angels, twelve names of Israel, twelve names of the Apostles, twelve foundations, twelve pearls, and the measurement of the wall of the city is twelve by twelve cubits. Twelve is the number which expresses government, and here we have the perfect government revealed.

This wall with its twelve gates, twelve angels, twelve names of the tribes of Israel, twelve foundations with the names of the Apostles of the Lamb, shows some kind of connection between the holy city, the Bride of the Lamb, and the earthly Jerusalem. (See Ezekiel xlviii: 31-34.) "The wall is what fences a city off from without; the gate is what gives it communication with that which is without. In that which marks the exclusive distinction of the Church the Apostles appear; in that which marks its relationship with the world the twelve tribes appear; for the Apostles are the foundation of the Church, whereas Israel is always God's first thought in His government of the world. In that which symbolizes the going forth of the Church's authority towards the world Israel therefore naturally comes into prominence."* The administration of Israel is from the heavenly city, which administration will rest in the hands of the twelve Apostles according to the promise of our Lord "ye shall sit upon twelve thrones judging the twelve tribes of Israel" (Matt. xix: 28). Then the twelve angels at the gates are, what angels always will be, ministering spirits. They are at the disposal of the Saints, who judge the world and angels (1 Cor. xi: 2-3). The twelve founda-

---

* T. B. Baines on Revelation

tions with the names of the twelve Apostles reminds us of Eph. ii: 20. "And are built upon the foundation of the Apostles and Prophets, Jesus Christ Himself being the chief corner stone." And it is a significant as well as blessed expression "the Apostles of the Lamb." The Lamb is the foundation of all. But the wall itself seems to represent symbolically Israel in her sphere of blessing to the millennial earth, standing between the heavenly and the earthly. No doubt there will be communication also between the earthly Jerusalem and the heavenly. It is well to confess our ignorance in all these matters. How little after all we know of the full meaning. When at last we shall be in that city with all the Saints, we shall know as we are known.

"And the city lieth four-square, and the length thereof is as great as the breadth; and he measured the city with the reed, twelve thousand furlongs. The length and breadth and the height of it are equal. And he measured the wall thereof, one hundred and forty and four cubits, according to the measure of a man, that is of an angel." The city is perfect in structure. It is described as being a cube. And by this is signified that it is the climax of perfection in the symmetry of its construction. Such will be the church in glory. That this city cannot be an earthly habitation is seen by its measurement. It is twelve thousand furlongs in length, breadth and height. Twelve thousand furlongs are fifteen hundred miles. This is beyond human comprehension. "In Ezekiel (describing the millennial Jerusalem) the city is large, becoming a splendid earthly metropolis; in Revelation the holy city is vast beyond all possible earthly limits. In Ezekiel it is of the quadrangular form, often used in Scripture to indicate perfect earthly symmetry; in Revelation there is another dimension, a height equal to the length and the breadth, showing a perfect cube, a still higher order of symmetry, heavenly in character, and manifestly unsuited to the earth."

"It is surely no mere coincidence that the Holy of holies in the temple was of the same cubic form. 'The oracle in the forepart was twenty cubits in length, and twenty cubits in breadth and twenty cubits in the height thereof: and he overlaid it with pure gold' (1 Kings vi: 20). Now David gave to Solomon 'the pattern of all that he had *by the Spirit* of the courts of the house of the Lord.' (1 Chron. xxviii: 12.) His plans therefore, like those of Moses, were formed after a heavenly model, and had a typical signification, so that the cubic form of the holiest place in the temple was an inspired type of the perfect symmetry of that 'habitation of God' which formed the pattern of these earthly structures. Here too the number of administrative perfection twice appears in the twelve thousand furlongs, which is the length of the side, and in the twelve times twelve, or one 'hundred and forty and four cubits,' of the height of the wall.

"The measure is 'the measure of a man, that is, of the angel.' The standard therefore is after the measure of man, not in his earthly body, but in the body he will have after resurrection, when he is clothed upon with his house which is from heaven. In these 'spiritual bodies' the 'children of the resurrection' are said to be 'equal unto the angels' (Luke xx: 36), and it is to this new condition that the standard of measurement is conformed. The scene, though all symbolic, is throughout symbolic of the heavenly, and not of the earthly. The symbols are, of course, borrowed from the earth, but each has a heavenly stamp impressed upon it."*

And the foundations were all adorned by precious stones and these twelve stones all tell out divine glory. The Jasper again stands first; the wall itself is of Jasper, while the first foundation stone mentioned is also Jasper. It stands for the Glory of God. Then the stones follow in their order. The Sapphire (blue); the Chalcedony (a combination of grey, blue and yellow); the Emerald (green); the Sardonyx (of a pale blue); the Sardius (bloodred); the Chrysolite (purple and green); the Beryl (bluish green); the Topaz (pale green or golden); the Chrysoprasus (mixed blue, green and yellow); the Jacinth (combination of red, violet and yellow), and the Amethyst (purple). And what must be the deeper meaning of all these precious stones! What varied aspects of the Glory of God they must represent! And the Redeemed in their heavenly city shall know, understand and enjoy it all. What wonderful, unspeakable glory is ahead of us! May we look forward to it every day and willingly serve and suffer the little while down here.

The city itself was seen by John as of pure gold. Gold typifies the righteousness of God in His nature and such the holy city is, composed of the Saints who were made through grace the partakers of the divine

---

* T. Baines

nature. "And the twelve gates were twelve pearls, each one of the several gates was of one pearl, and the street of the city was pure gold as it were transparent glass." How suitable the pearl to form each gate, the entrance to the city divine. The Pearl is a type of the Church. She is the one pearl of great price for which the Lord gave all He had (Matt. xiii: 45-46). And the golden street like unto pure glass shows that all the ways and walks in that city are according to righteousness and defilement is eternally impossible.

And there was no temple in that city; the Lord God Almighty and the Lamb are the temple of it. There is no need any longer of a certain access into the presence of God, as it was on earth, but there is a free and unhindered fellowship with God and with His ever blessed Son, the Lamb. Precious it is to hear Him again mentioned as the Lamb. His blessed work which He accomplished can never be forgotten by the Saints in Glory. And the light is not created light, but the light is the Glory of God and the lamp thereof is the Lamb. The Glory of God and Christ the Lamb of God will be the light and supersede all created light.

"And the nations shall walk by its light and the kings of the earth bring their glory and honor unto it*; and the gates of it shall not be shut at all by day for there shall be no night there. And they shall bring the glory and honor of the nations unto it." From this we learn that the glory light which shines eternally and undiminished in the holy city is the light in which the saved millennial nations on the earth walk. And the

---

* This is the better rendering.

kings of the earth bring their glory and honor unto it; not "into" as it is rendered in the Authorized Version. The heavens then rule, for Christ and His co-heirs are in that holy city, and the Government and rule over the earth proceeds from there. The kings bring their glory and honor unto it, they bow in homage in the presence of the holy city. Heaven is acknowledged as the source of all light, glory and blessing. When the nations and the kings of the earth go up to Jerusalem to worship the Lord of Hosts during the millennial age (Psalm lxxii: 8-11; Is. lx: 1-3; Zech. xiv: 16) we doubt not, they will turn their faces upward. Mount Zion in Israel's land will have resting upon it the glory and then above it the vision of the City in which the Glory dwells and from which the Glory emanates. And unto it they bring the honor and glory. The open gates, never closed, denote security and suggest also communication and intercourse with the earth. "There shall be no night there"; the night of sin and sorrow is forever gone for the dwellers in the holy city. "And there shall in no wise enter into it anything that defileth, neither whatsoever worketh abomination, or maketh a lie, but they which are written in the Lamb's book of life."

Chapter XXII. *The River and the Tree of Life. Verses 1-2.* "And he shewed me a pure river of water of life, bright as crystal, proceeding out of the throne of God and of the Lamb. In the midst of the street of it, and on either side of the river was the tree of life, bearing twelve manner of fruits, yielding its fruit every month, and the leaves of the tree were for the

healing of the nations." We must remember that
this is the heavenly Jerusalem, the holy city over the
earth. The Jerusalem on the earth in her millennial
glory has also a river of water. Ezekiel in his great
temple vision describes that stream. "Afterward he
brought me again unto the door of the house, and
behold waters issued out from under the threshold of
the house eastward" (Ez. xlvii: 1). And Zechariah in
his final vision, in the chapter in which we see "His
feet standing upon the Mount of Olives," tells of that
stream. "And it shall be in that day that living waters
shall go out from Jerusalem" (Zech. xiv: 8). That
stream of living water flowing forth from the earthly
Jerusalem is no doubt a real river of water, healing,
as it will, the waters of the Dead Sea. It also denotes
the spiritual blessings which will flow forth from
Jerusalem. But the pure river of water of life, bright
as crystal, in the heavenly Jerusalem does not proceed
from the temple, but from the throne of God and the
Lamb. The heavenly river is in the fullest sense of
the word the symbol of all life, blessing, joy, peace
and all the spiritual blessings the Saints possess and
enjoy. And when we examine Ezekiel xlvii again we
find something which corresponds with this vision of
the heavenly city. "And by the river upon the bank
thereof, on this side and on that side, shall grow
every tree for meat, whose leaf shall bring forth new
fruit according to his months, because their waters
issued out of the sanctuary, and the fruit thereof shall
be for meat, and the leaf thereof for healing" (Ezek.
xlvii: 12). We repeat, this will be in the Jerusalem on
the earth. Well has it been said "the earthly things

are moulded after the heavenly" (See Ex. xxv: 40;
xxvi: 30; xxvii: 8). The river on earth with its trees,
fruits and healing, is but a shadow of the tree of life,
bearing twelve manner of fruits, in the Jerusalem
above. The tree of life reminds us of Eden. It was
there, but Adam did not eat of it in his unfallen state
and when he became a transgressor by eating of the
tree of the knowledge of good and evil, the way to
the tree of life was barred by the Cherubim with the
flaming sword. Eating of that tree would have meant
for Adam to live forever as to the body.* And here
in the holy city the tree of life is seen and the
blessed fruit from it is eaten. The tree of the knowledge of good and evil is no longer seen. As another
has said "that tree whose taste brought death, was
withered up by the cross." And the millennial earth
receives the blessing from these glorious conditions
above. The light from above, as we saw, is the light
in which the millennial nations walk; the government
proceeds from above and the leaves of the tree of life
are for the healing of the nations. But the Saints
above eat the fruits of that tree. But what will this
all mean! Surely the half has not been told.

5. *The Seven Glories of the Redeemed. Verses 3-5.*
Unspeakably beautiful and glorious are the concluding
statements of this glory-section of the Revelation.
Seven glories of the Redeemed are enumerated.   1.
There will be no more curse. It means a perfect
sinlessness; perfect holiness. 2. The throne of God
and of the Lamb is there and the redeemed are forever

---

* He did not lose immortality of soul by his transgression.

linked with that throne. It is a perfect and blessed government which can never be disturbed by disorder. 3. His servants shall serve Him. Heaven will not consist in idleness. The holy city knows of service. And the service the Saints will render to God in glory will be a perfect service. What will it be? We do not know what service it will be. God will have many surprises for His Saints in glory. 4. There is also an eternal vision. "And they shall see His face." Oh! joy of all the joys in glory to see Him as He is and never lose sight of Him in all eternity. 5. His name shall be in their foreheads. It tells of eternal ownership and eternal possession. His name and the Glory connected with it will be ours in eternal ages. 6. An eternal day. No more night; no need of any light. He is the light for all eternity. 7. An eternal reign. And they shall reign forever and ever. What glory and blessedness all this means. Such are the coming glories of the Redeemed. Oh! the deceitfulness of sin and Satan's power to blind the eyes of humanity! They prefer to serve sin and the master who stands behind sin and despise such riches of glory which the grace of God offers in the Lord Jesus Christ to every sinner. Reader! what will be *your* home in eternity?

TENTH DIVISION. THE FINAL MESSAGES.

Chapter XXII: 6-21

Chapter XXII. *The Angel's Message. Verses 6-11.* The Prophetic Part of the Revelation is ended and the Epilogue, containing the final messages of the Book, remains to be considered. Once more the assurance is given that these sayings (words) are faithful and true. In chapter xxi: 5 God Himself had commanded to write for these words are faithful and true. Here it is an angel who speaks. "And the Lord God of the holy Prophets (literal: of the spirits of the Prophets) sent his angel to show unto His servants the things which must shortly be done." This reminds us of the beginning of the book, where we find a similar announcement. Suddenly some day these things will come to pass. The Lord will call His people to glory in a moment, in the twinkling of an eye, and then these things John had beheld will shortly come to pass. And then His own voice breaks in: "Behold I come quickly; Blessed is He that keepeth the sayings of the prophecy of this Book." Three times we find this announcement in the last chapter (verses 7, 12 and 20). Here it is connected with the walk of the believer. Just as in the beginning of the book a blessing is pronounced upon them that read the words of this prophecy (i: 3), so we have at the close of Revelation a similar beatitude. And keeping these blessed words means more than believing in them; their power is to shape our conduct and walk. What godly lives God's people would live on earth, what unselfish and sacrificing lives, if they remembered constantly Him who thus testifies three times in the last chapter of the Bible "Behold I come quickly." And the awful results in Christendom to-day for not having kept the sayings of the Prophecy of this Book. The nations to-day would not be fighting and killing as they do if they believed the sayings of this Prophecy. And John fell down to worship before the feet of the angel, who had been the instrument to show him these things. But this angel like the other angel in chapter xix: 10 refused the worship of the Apostle. The humility of angels is a forgotten truth. They have nothing of the crime of the devil, which is pride, in themselves; they honor and worship God and are jealous of His rights. What an answer to Romanism the angels are in their rejection of worship! Very foolishly some people have used the angel's words "Worship God" as an indication that the Lord Jesus should not be worshipped. One of these teachers approached the writer with this strange assertion and demanded scriptural proof that the Lord Jesus should be worshipped. We referred him to John v: 23. And he owes us still the reply to our letter.

Then the Seer is told not to seal the sayings of this Prophecy. Daniel was told to do the opposite (Dan. xii: 4). Old Testament prophecy reveals prophetic events in the far distance. They could then not be fully comprehended. But after Christ came and the full revelation of things to come is given, no sealing is needed; the events are at hand, yet grace has delayed and delays still the fulfillment. And the heavenly messenger announces also the fixed state of the two classes into which all humanity is divided. The unjust and filthy, the unsaved, continue to exist in the nature which they possess, and the fact that the desires of that corrupt nature can no longer be gratified must constitute in itself an unspeakable torment. The righteous and holy, those saved by grace, partakers of the divine nature will always be righteous and holy. Utterly false is it to teach, as it is being done, that the righteous are Christians who are justified, and the holy are the "believers who made a deeper experience." Every Christian who is justified by faith is also sanctified.

2. The Message of the Lord. Verses 12-13. And now the Lord speaks again. For the second time He announces His coming. Here it is in connection with rewards. "My reward is with Me." He Himself will receive His reward which is due Him as the sin-bearer. He will see the travail of His soul and be satisfied. And with His coming, His own people will receive their rewards. What a stimulating power His soon coming is to service! And the coming One is the Alpha and Omega, the first and the last, the beginning and the end.

3. The Two classes. Verses 14-15. Once more the two classes come into view. This is in fullest keeping with the end of the Book and the end of the Bible. The Authorized Version here is faulty. Instead of "Blessed are they that do His commandments" the correct reading is "Blessed are they that wash their robes." The former is an interpolation; the latter is the divine statement.* Eternal life and eternal glory cannot be obtained by keeping commandments, by the works of the law. The blood of the Lamb alone is the title to glory. And then the other class. The one who rejects Christ and thereby denies his lost condition and need of a Saviour, loveth and maketh a

---

* All leading scholars like Alford, Darby, etc., make the change. Even the Vulgate has it "Beati, qui lavant stolas suas in sanguinem Agni."

lie. He lives according to the old nature and the fruits of the flesh are there.

4. *The Final Testimony of Christ Concerning Himself. Verse 16.* How He speaks in this last Bible book! In the beginning of Revelation we find His self-witness in the church-message and once more we hear His voice, bearing testimony to Himself. How majestic, I, Jesus! He reveals Himself once more by the name of humiliation. What comfort it must have been to John! What comfort it is to us! Then He speaks of Himself as the Root and Offspring of David. He is David's Lord and David's son (Psalm cx: 1). He is the Hope of Israel and in Him the promises made to David will all be realized. This will be the case when He comes to reign in power and great glory. But He also speaks of Himself as "the bright and morning-star." His coming in power and glory is the sun-rise for Israel and the Gentiles, the breaking of the millennial day. But for His Church He comes first as the morning-star, as the morning-star in the eastern sky precedes the rising of the sun in all His glory. The Lord will come as the morning-star some time in the interval between the 69th and 70th week of Daniel and as the Sun of Righteousness after that week has come to an end.

5. *The Answer of the Spirit and the Bride. Verse 17.* As soon as He mentions Himself as the morning-star, there is an answer from the earth. The Spirit now down here, for He came down from heaven on Pentecost, and the Bride, the Church, say, "Come." It is addressed to the Lord. They both long for

His coming. And each individual believer who heareth
is asked to join in with this "Come." Surely in these
days of darkness and world-confusion, the Spirit
saith, "Come!" And never before were there so many
individual believers on earth who say "Come," who
wait for His coming. And the, Come—from loving
hearts will increase and become a loud and pleading
cry, till one blessed day He will answer and come
to take His waiting people home. Here also is the
final Gospel message of the Bible. He that will
let him take the water of life freely. Once more a
loving God makes it clear that the water of life is free
to all who want it. It is the last "Whosoever" in the
Bible.

6. The Final Warning. Verses 18-19. And what
a solemn warning is given! In a larger sense the warning applies to the entire Word of God. Higher criticism, which takes away, and false teachers, who add
unto it, find written here their deserved judgment.
But the Revelation is specially in view. Whosoever
meddles with His Revelation must fall under the
severest divine displeasure. Beware! oh ye critics!
Beware! ye who call this Book un-inspired and warn
against the study of it!

*7. The Final Message. The Final Prayer. The
Final Benediction. Verses 20-21.* We reach the final
statements of this great Book. For the third time He
announces His Coming. "He that testifieth these
things saith, surely I come quickly." It is the last
time our Lord speaks from heaven. The next time His
voice will be heard will be on that day when He

descends out of heaven with a shout. While the two former announcements of His coming found in this chapter are preceded by the word, "Behold," this last one affirms the absolute certainty of the event. And there is the answer, the blessed response. "Amen. Even so, come, Lord Jesus." It is the Church which answers His positive and certain announcement. It is the last word recorded in the Bible coming from the lips of man. The first word we hear man address to the Lord in the Bible is the solemn word "I heard thy voice in the garden, and I was afraid" (Gen. iii: 10). The last word addressed to the Lord by redeemed man is "even so, Come, Lord Jesus." And between these two utterances in Genesis and Revelation is the story of redemption. Well might this final prayer of the Bible be termed, the forgotten prayer. But it is equally true, with the revival of the study of prophecy, more hearts and lips are praying to-day for His Coming, than ever before. And the prayer will be answered. May the reader and the writer pray for His Coming daily and may our lives too bear witness to the fact that we expect Him to answer the petition of His people. The final benediction assures us once more of the Grace of our Lord Jesus Christ. The better rendering is "The Grace of our Lord Jesus Christ be with all the Saints." Grace in all its divine and never failing fullness will sustain all the Saints, till they are gathered into the Father's house.

Our task is finished. Humbly we put it into His hands and lay this exposition at His feet. If, it pleases Him to use it in making the future, coming things, and especially His own person and glory, a greater reality in the hearts and lives of His people, we shall forever praise Him.

APPENDIX I.

The Seventy-Week Prophecy*

Daniel ix: 24-27.

A Corrected Text of the Prophecy. The Authorized Version is somewhat incorrect. We give therefore first of all a corrected translation.

Seventy weeks are apportioned out upon thy people and upon the holy city to finish the transgression and to make an end of sins, and to cover iniquity, and to bring in the righteousness of the ages, and to seal the vision and prophet, and to anoint the holy of holies. Know therefore and understand: From the going forth of the word to restore and to rebuild Jerusalem unto Messiah, the Prince, shall be Seven Weeks and Sixty-two Weeks. The street and the wall shall be built again, even in troublous times. And after the Sixty-two Weeks shall Messiah be cut off, and shall have nothing; and the people of the prince that shall come shall destroy the city and the sanctuary; and the end thereof shall be with an overflow, and unto the end war, the desolations determined. And he shall confirm a covenant with the many for one week; and in the midst of the week he shall cause the sacrifice and the oblation to cease and because of the protection of abominations there shall be a desolator, even until the consummation and what is determined shall be poured out upon the desolator (verses 24-27).

What are the Seventy Weeks? To many readers of the Book of Daniel it is not quite clear what the expression "seventy weeks" means, and when it is stated that each week represents a period of seven years,

---

* This Prophecy is of such importance in the Study of Revelation that we quote the exposition as given in our Book on Daniel.

many Christians do not know why such is the case. A brief word of explanation may therefore be in order. The literal translation of the term "seventy weeks" is "seventy sevens." Now this word "sevens" translated "weeks" may mean "days" and it may mean "years." What then is meant here, seventy times seven days or seventy times seven years? It is evident that the "sevens" mean year weeks, seven years to each prophetic week. Daniel was occupied in reading the books and in prayer with the seventy years of the Babylonian captivity. And now Gabriel is going to reveal to him something which will take place in "seventy sevens," which means seventy times seven years. The proof that such is the case is furnished by the fulfillment of the prophecy itself. Now seventy times seven years makes 490 years.

What is to be Accomplished? Verse 24 gives the great things, which are to be accomplished during these seventy year weeks of 490 years. They are the following: (1) To finish the transgression. (2) To make an end of sins. (3) To cover iniquity. (4) To bring in the righteousness of ages. (5) To seal the vision and prophet. (6) To anoint the Holy of Holies.

Now it must be borne in mind that these things concern exclusively Daniel's people and not Gentiles but the holy city Jerusalem. It is clear that the finishing of transgression, the end of sins and the covering of iniquity has a special meaning for Israel as a nation. The foundation upon which this future work of Grace for His earthly people rests is the death of Christ. Our blessed Lord "died for that nation" as He also died for us who are sinners of the Gentiles (John xi: 50). Up to now the transgression of the Jewish people is not yet finished, nor is for them "an end made of sins." The death of Christ has made this possible for the nations, but before it becomes applied this period of time, 490 years, must have passed, and when they are accomplished the transgression of His people will be finished and all the other blessings will come upon them. That will be according to other Scriptures when the times of the Gentiles end and when the Son of Man, the rejected One, appears the second time. Then "He shall turn away ungodliness from Jacob" and "will take away their sins" (Rom. xi: 26-27). Many passages in the prophetic Word reveal the same promises of national cleansing and forgiveness, into which we cannot enter more fully. We see at once that the blessings promised here to Daniel's people and to the holy city refer us to the time when the Son of Man is manifested, the time when the remnant of the nation shall look upon Him whom they have pierced (Zech. xii).

And the same time when God will be merciful to His people and cover their iniquity "the righteousness of or eternal justification or righteousness of the ages" will be brought in. This means the beginning of that age of blessing, which in the New Testament is called "the dispensation of the fullness of times" (Ephes. i: 10), in which the King shall reign in righteousness. Then righteousness will be established on this earth and the holy city, as Gabriel calls Jerusalem, will not only be a sharer of the blessings and glory, but will herself be righteous. It is written of Jerusalem "afterward thou shalt be called, The City of righteousness" (Isaiah i: 26). Still greater is Jeremiah's word he received from the Lord concerning that day when the righteousness of the ages has come.

Behold, the days come, saith the Lord, that I will perform that good thing which I have promised unto the house of Israel and to the house of Judah. In those days, and at that time, will I cause the Branch of righteousness to grow up unto David; and he shall execute Judgment and righteousness in the land. In those days shall Judah be saved, and Jerusalem shall dwell safely and this is the name wherewith she shall be called, The Lord our righteousness (Jeremiah xxxiii, 14-16).

The vision and prophecy will be sealed, that is accredited, because their final accomplishment has been reached in these events of blessings for God's earthly people. Also the Holy of Holies will be anointed, a statement which many have applied to our Lord. It has nothing whatever to do with Him, but it is the anointing of the Holy of Holies in another temple, which will stand in the midst of Jerusalem. Of this great millennial temple the prophetic Word is not silent. The other prophet of the captivity, Ezekiel, had a vision of this temple and its worship.

It is of the greatest importance to grasp the thought that these things have nothing to do with Gentiles or with the Church. They concern Daniel's people, the Jews and Jerusalem. If this had been understood the commentators would not have made that mistaken interpretation of the seventy weeks prophecy which is so universally taught in our day. We shall touch upon these errors in the course of our exposition.

The Division of the Seventy Weeks. After the general announcement of the seventy sevens and what is to be accomplished for Jerusalem and Daniel's people when this prophetic period of time expires, Gabriel gives further information to the Prophet. This information is introduced by the exhortation to know and to understand or to discriminate. What follows is the division of the seventy weeks into three parts. The first part consists of seven year weeks, that is 49 years. The second part consists of sixty-two weeks or 434 years, then there is one week, the seventieth, left, which gives us the third part.

The Beginning of the Seventy Weeks. We have to ascertain in examining the prophetic history of these different divisions when the seventy year weeks began. If we were to touch upon the different views and explanations, which have been made on this point we would have to fill numerous pages. One is reminded of Job xxxviii: 2 in reading the theories of commentators, "Who is this that darkeneth counsel by words without knowledge?" The text is very plain. We read the definite beginning in verse 25. It is when the command was to be given to restore and build Jerusalem. From that time to Messiah the Prince are to be seven weeks and sixty-two weeks, that is 483 years. These seventy year weeks should not be reckoned from the time Daniel prayed nor from the time Cyrus gave permission for the people to return and to build the temple. In Ezra, chapter i, we read that it was in

the first year of Cyrus, King of Persia, that the Lord
stirred him up, whose coming and work Isaiah had announced long before his birth. Significant is the
proclamation, which Cyrus sent forth. But it has only
to do with the building of the temple in Jerusalem.
"The Lord of heaven has given me all the kingdoms
of the earth; and He hath charged me to build Him a
house at Jerusalem, which is in Judah." But this edict
is not the starting point of the seventy year weeks, for
they are to begin with the word to restore and build
the city itself. But in the Book of Ezra also we find in
chapter vii what happened in the reign of Artaxerxes,
King of Persia, known in history as Artaxerxes Longi-
manus. In the seventh year of his reign another edict
was issued, but a careful reading will show that that
was not the command to restore and build Jerusalem.
We have to turn to the second chapter of Nehemiah
for the beginning of these seventy year weeks. It was
in the twentieth year of the reign of Artaxerxes that
the command was given to restore and to build Jerusalem. From that time the seventy year weeks must be
reckoned. This twentieth year of Artaxerxes was the
year 445 B. C., which is proven historically. The year
is not only mentioned in Nehemiah ii but also the
month. It was in Nisan. The seventy year weeks
began therefore in the month of Nisan 445 B. C.

When we read that "the street and the wall shall be
built again, even in troublous times" and then up to the
time when Messiah is to be cut off, it should be sixty-
two year weeks (434 years), we have the time revealed
that it would take to restore the city, namely seven
year weeks, forty-nine years.

A remarkable prediction. We have then before us a remarkable prediction. The exact time of the first advent of Christ is here predicted when Messiah the Prince, He who is the Hope of His people Israel, should appear. But still more remarkable is the fact that a certain event of His life on earth is predicted. It is not His birth which is to take place after the expiration of the sixty-nine year weeks, but He is to be "cut off and shall have nothing." It is a prediction of His death on the cross. It remains to be seen if this has found its literal fulfillment and if Messiah died at the time when the 483 years reckoned from the month Nisan 445 B. C. had expired. Before we do so we must call here attention to the critics of the Book of Daniel and their methods.

Because the critics do not want to believe that it is possible to predict far off events, such as are written in Daniel, the career and death of Alexander, the work of Antiochus Epiphanes and others, they invent an imaginary pious Jew who wrote the Book of Daniel after Antiochus Epiphanes had been on the scene. Now if this were true and such a "pious Jew" and not Daniel wrote this book, how can it be explained that after all there is a prediction made which clearly points to the death of Christ and which also outlines the result upon the city of Jerusalem, that the people of the Prince to come are to destroy the city and the sanctuary? These gentlemen, whose habit is to deny, solved the difficulty here by denying absolutely that the person called "Messiah the Prince" is Christ. What dishonest methods, juggling and twisting of words,

they have used to reach this conclusion would be amus-
ing, if it were not so sad. Chief among those is Canon
Farrar on Daniel. We quote from this book:

> "An anointed one shall be cut off." There can be no
> reasonable doubt that this is a reference to the deposition
> of the high priest Onias III, and his murder by Adronicus
> (B. C.), This startling event is mentioned in 2 Macc. iv: 34,
> and by Josephus, and in Daniel xi: 22. It is added "and
> no......to him." Perhaps the word "helper" (xi: 45) has
> fallen out of the text, as Graetz supposes; or the words
> may mean "there is no (priest) for it (the people)." The
> A. V. renders it "but not for himself"; and in the margin
> "and shall have nothing"; or "and they (the Jews) shall
> be no more his people." The R. V. renders it "and shall
> have nothing." I believe with Dr. Joel that, in the Hebrew
> words "veeyn lo" there may be a sort of cryptographic
> allusion to the name Onias. "The people of the coming
> prince shall devastate the city and the sanctuary (translation
> uncertain). This is an obvious allusion to the destruction
> and massacre inflicted on Jerusalem by Appolonius and the
> army of Antiochus Epiphanes (B. C. 167), Antiochus is
> called the prince that shall come "because he was at Rome
> when Onias III was murdered."

But enough of this; the way these men try to avoid
the truth and by their reasoning methods try to get rid
of everything God's people have believed in the past, is
sufficient to show what spirit stands behind them.

The Evidence that "Messiah the Prince" is Christ.
The question then is do the words "Messiah the
Prince" the One who is to be cut off and nothing for
him, really mean Christ or some other anointed one,
as the critics claim? The evidence that it is the Lord
Jesus Christ is furnished in the most remarkable ful-

fillment of the prophecy in the time when our Lord came to Jerusalem the last time before His passion. Exactly 483 years after the command to restore and build Jerusalem had been given, the Lord Jesus Christ entered into Jerusalem to present Himself and His claims; a few days after that He was nailed to the cross. This has been shown in a perfect chronological way so that it is beyond even the shadow of a doubt. We give an extract from "Daniel in the Critics' Den" which shows this fact.

If, therefore, the vision be a Divine prophecy, an era of "Sixty-nine weeks" that is 483 prophetic years, reckoned from the 14th of March, B. C. 445, should close with the public presentation and death of "Messiah the Prince." No student of the Gospels can fail to see that the Lord's last visit to Jerusalem was not only in fact, but in intention the crisis of His ministry. From the time that the accredited leaders of the nation had rejected His Messianic claims, He had avoided all public recognition of those claims. But now His testimony had been fully given, and the purpose of His entry into the capital was to openly proclaim His Messiahship and to receive His doom. Even His apostles themselves had again and again been charged that they should not make Him known; but now He accepted the acclamations of the whole multitude of the disciples. And when the Pharisees protested, He silenced them with the indignant rebuke, "I tell you that if these should hold their peace the stones would immediately cry out." These words can only mean that the divinely appointed time had arrived for the public announcement of His Messiahship, and that the Divine purpose could not be thwarted. The full significance of the words which follow is lost in our Authorized Version. As the cry was raised by His disciples, "Hosanna to the Son of David, blessed is the King of Israel that cometh in the Name of the Lord."

He looked off towards the Holy City and exclaimed, "If thou also hadst known, even ON THIS DAY, the things that belong to thy peace—but now they are hid from thine eyes!" The nation had already rejected Him, but this was the fateful day when their decision must be irrevocable. And we are expressly told that it was the fulfillment of prophecy, "Shout O daughter of Jerusalem; behold thy King cometh unto thee." It was the only occasion on which His kingly claims were publicly announced.

And no other day in all His ministry will satisfy the words of Daniel's vision. And the date of that first "Palm Sunday" can be ascertained with certainty. No year in the whole field of ancient history is more definitely indicated than that of the beginning of our Lord's public ministry. According to the Evangelist it was "the fifteenth year of Tiberius Cæsar" (Luke iii: 1). Now the reign of Tiberius, as beginning from August 19, A. D. 14, was as well known a date in the time of Luke as the reign of Queen Victoria is in her own day. The Evangelist, moreover, with a prophetic anticipation of the perverseness of expositors and "reconcilers" goes on to name six prominent public men as holding specified positions in the fifteenth year of Tiberius, and each one of these is known to have actually held the position thus assigned to him in the year in question. As, therefore, the first Passover of the Lord's ministry was that of Nisan, A. D. 29, the date of the Passion is thus fixed by Scripture itself. For it is no longer necessary to offer proof that the crucifixion took place at the fourth Passover of the ministry. According to the Jewish custom, our Lord went up to Jerusalem on the 8th Nisan, which, as we know, fell that year upon a Friday. And having spent the Sabbath at Bethany, He entered the Holy City the following day, as recorded in the Gospels. The Julian date of that 10th Nisan was Sunday the 6th of April, A. D. 32. What then was the length of the period intervening between the issuing of the decree to rebuild Jerusalem and this public advent of "Messiah the Prince"—between the 14th of March, B. C. 445, and the 6th of April A. D. 32 (when He entered into Jerusalem). THE

INTERVAL WAS EXACTLY AND TO THE VERY
DAY 173,880 DAYS, OR SEVEN TIMES SIXTY-NINE
PROPHETIC YEARS OF 360 DAYS. *

Here then is perfect evidence that "Messiah the
Prince," who was to be "cut off and shall have nothing" is our Lord Jesus Christ, for He appeared in Jerusalem on exactly the day on which the sixty-nine
prophetic weeks expired and a few days later He was
put to death on the Cross. No wonder the critics invent all kinds of schemes and interpretations to get
rid, so to speak, of this powerful evidence of revelation.

The Hebrew phrase "veeyn lo" translated in the
Authorized Version, but not for Himself, is better
rendered by "and shall have nothing." It has been in-

---

* From B. C. 445 to A. D. 32 is 476 years = 173,740 days
(476 x 365) + 116 days for leap years. And from 14th March
to 6th April, (reckoned inclusively according to Jewish
practice) is 24 days. But 173,746 + 116 + 24 = 173,880. And
69 x 7 x 360 = 173,880.

It must be borne in mind here that in reckoning years
from B. C. to A. D. one year must always be omitted; for,
of course, the interval between B. C. 1 and A. D. 1 is not
two years but one year. In fact B. C. 1 ought to be called
B. C. 0; and it is so described by astronomers, with whom
B. C. 445 is 444. And again, as the Julian year is 11 m.
10.46 s., or about the 129th part of a day, longer than the
mean solar year, the Julian calendar has three leap years too
many in every four centuries. This error is corrected by the
Gregorian reform, which reckons three secular years out of
four as common years. For instance, 1700, 1800, and 1900
were common years, and 2000 will be a leap year.

terpreted in different ways. We believe it means that
He did not receive then the Messianic kingdom. He
was rejected by His own and received not that which
belongs to Him.

The Destruction of the City Predicted. Linked with
the cutting off of Messiah is another remarkable
prophecy. "And the people of the prince that shall
come shall destroy the city and the sanctuary; and the
end thereof shall be with an overflow, and unto the end
war—the desolations determined." Judgment according to this is to overtake the city which rejected
the Messiah and both the city and the Temple were to
be destroyed. This work was to be done "by the people
of the prince that shall come." The prince of course
is not "Messiah the Prince," it is a prince that shall
come. But he himself is not to destroy the city and
the sanctuary, but the people from whose midst that
coming prince is to arise, will do the destructive work.
Now, the people who are here in view, are the Romans.
Out of the Roman empire there shall arise in the future
a prince. This prince or chief of the fourth empire is
identical with the little horn of Daniel vii. Once more
the head of the restored Roman empire as it is to be
during the time of the end looms up before us in the
last two verses of this chapter. The people of the coming prince, the Romans, were to come and destroy
both city and temple, after Messiah had been cut off
and had nothing for Himself. And this came to pass
as everybody knows. Our Lord had predicted this
doom of Jerusalem and had wept over it as He beheld
the awful doom in store for the city. The Jews had

anticipated what would come, for the chief priests and Pharisees declared "The Romans will come and take away both our palace and our nation" (John xi: 48). The Romans under Titus Vespasianus in the year seventy fulfilled this prediction and in that year the prophecy before us became history. But Titus is not "the prince that shall come."

The Future of the Jews Foretold. Another prophecy is linked with the one just examined. "The end thereof shall be with an overflow, and unto the end war—the desolations determined." These words give us the history of the Jewish people, of their land and their city, up to the present time. It is identical with what our Lord said, "and they shall fall by the edge of the sword and shall be led away captive into all nations; and Jerusalem shall be trodden down of the Gentiles until the times of the Gentiles are fulfilled (Luke xxi: 24). Both the prediction as communicated to Daniel by Gabriel and the words of our Lord tell of what is to be the lot of the Jews and of Jerusalem throughout this present age, till the end of the times of the Gentiles has been reached. History gives the answer about the fulfillment of these words.

The Seventieth Year Week. We have found up to this point that sixty-nine weeks of 483 years of the seventy year weeks are past. But what about the remaining seven years, the seventieth week? The last verse of Chapter ix tells us of that one week. It has not yet come, but still lies in the future.

The course of the seventy year weeks was interrupted by the rejection of Messiah the Prince, who came to His own and they received Him not. With this event, as we have seen, the sixty-ninth week closed and an indefinite period of unreckoned time follows; when that is expired the last prophetic week of seven years will begin and run its appointed course.

A close scrutiny of the twenty-sixth verse will make this clear. While we know that the Messiah was cut off immediately upon the close of the sixty-ninth week, nothing is said about the time when the destruction of the city and the sanctuary should take place. History tells us it transpired thirty-eight years after the death of Christ. Wars should continue to the end, but not a word is said when that end is to come. The one week, that is the seventieth week, is mentioned in the verse which follows this prediction, it comes, therefore, after this long interval has terminated.

This unreckoned period of time at the close of the sixty-ninth week has already lasted almost 1900 years. During this time the Jewish people have been scattered among all the nations of the earth and the predicted miseries written in their own law and in the prophets have been fulfilled in every generation. Yet God has preserved them not alone physically but also as a distinct race, even as our Lord announced when He spoke of the events of the last week of Daniel in His Olivet Discourse (Matthew xxiv). "This generation (race) shall not pass away till these things be fulfilled."

During this unreckoned period of time God has made known by revelation the blessed mystery of eternity, a mystery not made known in other ages, concerning the Church. There is now being gathered out from the nations a people for His Name and the Church is still building. The Gospel is being heralded world-wide. The heavens, however, are closed and this unreckoned period of time leading up to the end of the times of the Gentiles runs its appointed course. As we do not write on this present and, in the Old Testament, unrevealed age and its characteristics, we must turn our attention to the events recorded in verse 27.

Who Confirms a Covenant? The first thing we read is "And he shall confirm a (not the) covenant with the many for one week." We must remind ourselves again that all we read here concerns, as did the previous sixty-nine weeks, Daniel's people, the Jews, When the last week of seven years begins, preceding the time of ultimate blessing for the Jewish people, one will make a covenant with the mass of Jews. The question arises, who then is this person and what is the covenant he makes?

We mentioned before an erroneous view, which holds that everything predicted in these seventy weeks has been fulfilled in the past. The view holds that Messiah the Prince, the one who was cut off, is our Lord. However, the teaching is that "the prince that shall come" is also Christ and that it is Christ Himself who confirms the covenant in the last week. We quote Dr. Pusey who delivered a series of very learned lectures on Daniel at Oxford, and whose book on Daniel is considered an authority:

Not *in*, but *after*, these Sixty-two weeks, it is said, Messiah shall be cut off. Then follows the subdivision of the last week (verse 27) or seven years, wherein he was to be cut off, and yet not in the Sixty-nine weeks. He shall make then a covenant with many for one week and in the midst of the week he shall cause the sacrifice and oblation to cease.*

The Lord Jesus Christ is believed to be the one who makes the covenant. The cessation of the sacrifice and obligation in the midst of the week is explained as having been accomplished by His death on the cross. But such a view is altogether untenable. According to this widely accepted theory Christ made a covenant for seven years. Where is this stated elsewhere in Scripture? Nowhere is there even a hint that Christ was to confirm a covenant with many for seven years, but His covenant is an everlasting one. The error springs from the fact that the future of the Jewish people is not considered and the teaching of what is yet to be in the time of the end is completely passed by.

The one who confirms the covenant with the many for one week is "the prince that shall come" of verse 26. The prince that shall come, as we have seen, rises from the people who destroyed the city and the sanctuary, the Roman people. The prince that shall come is the dreadful little horn on the fourth beast (the Roman empire), the great head of the Roman empire seen as the Beast out of the Sea in Revelation xiii. When the last seven years, so pregnant with Jewish events, begins, the first thing will be that the Jews look

---

* Pusey, Daniel, page 176.

for protection to the great Man, who as a mighty prince controls the affairs of the Roman empire brought together under him as head. The aim of the Jews is to repossess Palestine, to have a Jewish state and to gain possession of the city of Jerusalem, so that they may be able to have a temple and their sacrificial ceremonies again. Zionism is the step towards such a restoration in unbelief, the first beginning of it. This coming prince, the beast, will take the Jews and their desires into consideration, perhaps he needs them too in the beginning of his career. He will make a covenant with them and under this covenant, most likely, they will be permitted to possess Palestine and to build a temple in Jerusalem. He will also promise them protection against any outside foes, especially the one who threateningly arises in the North, the Assyrian of Prophecy.

This covenant the Roman prince will make with the many, not with all the Jews. Throughout the prophetic Word we find the clearest evidence of a remnant of Jews, who trusting in the Lord, will see through this wicked prince and refuse to have anything whatever to do with that covenant. Isaiah xxviii 15 and 18 speak of this covenant. It is there called a covenant with death and an agreement with hell. In the Revelation this faithful remnant is seen witnessing and suffering and refusing to worship the Beast. All this we have learned in our exposition.

After the first three and one-half years of this last prophetic week are gone, he will break the covenant by causing the sacrifice and oblation to cease. From the Book of Revelation we learn that at that time he will become possessed by the power of Satan. In fellowship with the second beast, the false prophet, the personal Anti-Christ, who is in Jerusalem, he introduces idolatry and the most awful blasphemies among the Jews. All the temple ceremonials, sacrifices and oblations will have to be abandoned. The apostate nations will accept the Anti-christ as their Messiah and king and fall in line with his blasphemies. Then the character of the little horn and what was said of him will fully come out. "He shall speak great words against the most High, and shall wear out the Saints of the most High (the Jews who refused to enter his covenant), and think to change times and laws, and they shall be given into his hands until a time and times and the dividing of time." (Three and one-half years —Daniel vii: 25.) "And there was given unto him a mouth speaking great things and blasphemies, and power was given unto him to continue forty-two months" (Rev. xiii: 5). This shows the work he will do for 1,260 days, forty-two months, three and one-half years, the last half of the seventieth week. The part of the personal Anti-christ in these 1,260 days and three and one-half years is described in Rev. xiii: 11-17. An image of the first beast, the wicked head of the Roman power will be set up and the great idol endued with supernatural, satanic power must be worshipped under the penalty of death. Anti-christ himself, this wicked counterfeit of the true Christ, takes a place in the temple of God and by lying wonders shows himself that he is God and exalting himself above all

that is God and that is worshipped. Then the great
tribulation will be in force and the Jewish faithful
remnant will pass through the deepest waters of suffering.

We have still something unexplained in the last
verse of our chapter. We read "and because of the
protection (lit, wing) of abominations there shall be
a desolator, even until the consummation and what is
determined shall be poured out upon the desolator."
We shall not weary our readers with giving them the
different views and opinions on this seemingly difficult
passage. The abominations mentioned are idols and
idol worship. The protection, or wing, of these idols
is sought by the people and God is completely forgotten
and set aside by the apostate masses, who bow before
the Anti-christ. The fulfillment of the words of our
Lord in Matthew has come:

When the unclean spirit is gone out of a man, he walketh
through dry places, seeking rest, and findeth none. Then he
saith, I will return into my house from whence I came out;
and when he is come, he findeth it empty, swept, and gar-
nished. Then goeth he, and it taketh with himself seven
other spirits more wicked than himself, and they enter in
and dwell there; and the last state of that man is worse
than the first. Even so shall it be also unto this wicked
generation (Matt. xii: 43-45).

The wicked spirit, idolatry, will take hold of them
and they will be swept along into the worse blasphemies and worship Satan's masterpiece. On account of this abomination "there shall be a desolator,"
one who desolates the land. This desolator will con-

tinue to plague the Jews from the outset, while the
Anti-christ is with them in Jerusalem. The desolator
will devastate the land and conquer Jerusalem till the
consummation is reached. The consummation is the
close of the seven years. When that is reached the
desolator himself will be dealt with in judgment as well
as the two beasts. Who is the desolator? The King
of the North, the Assyrian of the endtime; he is the
one of whom we read in the previous chapter and
whose terrible work against the apostate nation is here
once more touched upon as falling into the second half
of the last prophetic week.

It is interesting to compare the two New Testament
records which give a large vision of the events of the
seven years which are in store for Daniel's people and
the Holy City, before the full blessing for the remnant
of this people and for Jerusalem can come. These
records are Matthew xxiv and that part of Revelation
which treats of these coming events, chapters vi-xix.
The reader will find this followed out in our exposition
of the Gospel of Matthew.*

And how far is the beginning of this last week of
Daniel from our time? No one can give an answer.
God only knows how soon all will come to pass. However, there is a sign present with us which is very significant. It is the restoration movement of the Jews
and their inability to carry out the plans and schemes
for their complete restoration. They are waiting for
"the Prince that shall come." It behooves us to wait

---

* Gospel of Matthew by A. C. G.

and watch. The days of God's Saints may be very few on earth. The last and next great event in the un-reckoned period of time, between the sixty-ninth and seventieth week, is the coming of the Lord for His Saints and this is imminent.

APPENDIX II.

Prominent Names and Their Symbolical Meaning in Revelation.

Abandon. Chapter ix: 11. Destruction. The King over the Locust army, denoting Satan and his agencies.

Abyss, The. ix: 1; xx: 1-3. The pit of the abyss or the deep. This expression occurs seven times in Revelation. Out of the deep, the lowest pit, there comes the demon and into the pit of the abyss Satan will be cast for 1,000 years. The Lake of Fire is a different place.

Accuser, The. Satan is the accuser of the Brethren. xii: 10. His expulsion out of heaven occurs in the middle of the week, followed by the great tribulation on earth.

Alpha. The first letter in the Greek alphabet; Omega is the last letter. Therefore Alpha and Omega is equivalent to an A and Z. Symbolical of the first and the last. i: 8; xxi: 6; xxii: 13.

Amen, The. A name of our Lord. He is the "verily," the truth, and assurance and certainty are expressed by this word. i: 14.

Angels. Angels are prominently mentioned throughout Revelation. The exposition shows that the angel mentioned in viii: 1-5; x: 1 is the Lord Jesus Christ. Angels will be used in the end of the age to carry out the decreed judgments. On the angels of the different churches, the symbolical meaning, see the exposition chapter i: 20.

The angels are the messengers who carried the Lord's message to the churches. They needed the power of the Spirit to do it. Hence the churches were to hear what the Spirit said to the churches. Rev. ii : 7, etc.

Anti-christ, The. The final and personal Anti-christ is mentioned for the first time in Revelation in chapter xiii : 11-18. He is also called the false Prophet, because he heads up the ecclesiastical corruption and apostasy of the end of the age. He must not be confounded with the first Beast out of the Sea who is a political head, the emperor of the revived Roman empire, the little horn of Daniel vii, and the Prince that shall come of Dan. ix : 26.

Antipas. An unknown faithful martyr in Pergamos, known to Christ. ii : 13, meaning one against all.

Apollyon. ix : 11. The Greek name of Abaddon, the King over the Locust army. The name means Destruction or Destroyer.

Ark, The. Chapter ix : 19. It is seen by John in the temple. It means symbolically the assured presence of Jehovah with His people Israel, the faithful remnant, in the trying times of Jacob's trouble.

Armageddon. Mentioned for the first time in the parenthesis between the sixth and seventh vial. Chap. xvi : 12-16. It means "The hill of slaughter." The battle of Armageddon will be of brief duration. It is the stone of Nebuchadnezzar's dream smiting suddenly the ten toes, the ten kingdoms (Dan. ii). The battle of Armageddon is briefly described in chapter xix : 19-20.

Alleluia. "Praise ye the Lord." The four Halle-lujahs are found in chapter xix: 1-5.

Babylon. On the literal and mystical Babylon see exposition of chapter xvii. The literal Babylon will undoubtedly be restored as a city of influence. But the city mentioned in chapter xvii is not the literal Babylon, but Rome. Not only will the Roman empire be revived, *but* also papal Rome. Babylon the great, the mother of Harlots, will see a great revival. The system in its corruption is described in chapter xviii.

Balaam. The heathen Prophet who could not curse Israel, but put a stumbling-block before the children of Israel. Used in Revelation to describe the corruption in the professing church in giving up the divinely demanded separation from the world. Chapter ii: 14.

Beast, The. The expression "four Beasts in Rev. iv and v, etc., is faulty. The correct rendering is "the four living Creatures" or the "four living ones." The term "Beast" applies to the revived Roman empire and its head, the little horn of Daniel, also called Beast in Daniel's vision. The Anti-christ is likewise called a Beast. The work of the two Beasts is seen in chapter xiii.

Birds, unclean and hateful. Symbolical of evil persons outwardly professing to be something but full of corruption. They describe the apostate masses of Christendom. Rev. xviii: 2. Also Matt. xiii: 31-32.

Black Horse. The black horse comes into view with the opening of the third seal. Black is the color of night, darkness and death.

Blood, with Hail and Fire. Chapter viii: 7. Not literal things, but symbols of divine judgment for this earth.

Bow, The. Chapter vi: 1. The bow without an arrow as in possession by the rider upon the white horse is the symbol of a bloodless conquest.

Bride, The. xxi: 2. The Bride of Christ, the Lamb's wife, xix: 7; it is not Israel but the church.

Brimstone and Fire. The symbols of divine wrath. Isa. xxx: 33.

Candlestick, Golden. Symbolical of that which gives light. Representing the seven assemblies. The church is on earth to give light.

Crowns. The symbols of given glory and also rewards for service. The crowns seen upon the seven heads of the dragon (xii: 3) and upon the four horns of the Beast (xiii: 1) denote despotic authority.

David, Key of. Symbolical of the right to open and to enter in. See Isa. xxii: 22. It is a prediction concerning Christ. The authority of the kingdom of heaven.

David, Root and offspring. xxii: 16. Christ is the Root and offspring of David.

Demons. Fallen spiritual beings; the wicked spirits over which Satan is the head. They will be worshipped by the apostates during the end of the age. Demon-worship is even now going on to some extent, for the anti-christian cults are produced by demons. (1 Tim. iv: 1.) See Rev. ix: 20-21. The word devils must be changed to demons. There is but one Devil, but legions of demons.

Dwellers on the Earth. This class mentioned repeatedly in Revelation are the large number of professing Christians, who did not receive the love of the truth and rejecting the Gospel follow the strong delusion and are utterly blinded, as well as hardened, during the tribulation.

Eagle. viii: 13. The word angel must be changed to "eagle." Symbolical of the coming judgment, as an eagle is a bird of prey. Eagle's wings (xii: 13-17) are symbolical of swift motion, escape and deliverance.

Earth. The prophetic territory of the Roman empire is mostly described by this form, though the entire earth is also indicated.

Earthquake. Symbolical of the shaking of all political and ecclesiastical institutions. But, as we show in our exposition, literal earthquakes will take place.

Elders, Twenty-four. The twenty-four elders typify all the redeemed in Glory. Old and New Testament Saints are included. After chapter xix this term does not appear again, because the church, the bride of Christ, is then seen separate from the entire company of the redeemed, and takes her exalted position as the Lamb's wife.

Eternal State, The. The eternal state is described in chapter xxi: 1-8.

Euphrates. This great river is mentioned twice in Revelation, ix: 14 and xvi: 12. It is the boundary line of the Roman empire and the land of Israel. See exposition of these passages.

Everlasting Gospel. xiv: 6. The declaration of the

Gospel of the Kingdom during the tribulation, and the proclamation of God as Creator to the heathen nations of the world, to prepare them for the gospel of the kingdom.

Fire. Often mentioned in this book and symbolical of the judgments which will be executed upon the earth as well as the everlasting wrath upon the unsaved.

Fornication. Spiritual wickedness in departing from the Truth of God, followed by the literal lusts of the flesh. The days of Lot will be on the earth before the Son of Man cometh.

Four. This number appears a number of times in Revelation. Four living creatures; four corners of the earth; four horns of the golden altar; four angels; four winds. Four is the number of universality.

Frogs. Mentioned between the sixth and seventh vial. Symbolical of demon influences, denoting filthy and wicked things. Frogs come out of slimy and dark waters; evil doctrines.

Glass, Sea of. Chapter iv: 6. Compare with Exod. xxx: 18-21 and 1 Kings vii: 23, etc. Symbolical of fixed lasting holiness. No more water needed for cleansing from sin, for the Saints in Glory are delivered from the presence of sin itself.

God, Supper of. Chapter xix: 17. Symbolical of God's judgment upon the wicked nations and the earth dwellers.

Gold. Symbolical of divine righteousness.

Grass. viii: 7. Symbolical of human prosperity. Isa. xl: 7 and 1 Peter i: 24.

Hades. The region of disembodied spirits; literally "the unknown." Christ has the Keys, and Hades with Death, because they came into existence through sin, will be cast into the Lake of fire.

Harvest of the Earth. The harvest is the end of the age. In chapter xiv: 14-15 we read of the Lord's judgment dealing with the earth.

Hidden Manna. ii: 17. Symbolical of the reward those who overcome will receive from the Lord.

Horns. Horn is symbolical of power. Horns mean typically kings, powers and kingdoms. Dan. vii: 24.

Image of the Beast. xiii: 12-15. Compare with Dan. iii. It will be a literal image of the princely leader of the revived Roman empire, the first Beast, which John saw rising out of the sea.

Islands. Mentioned under the sixth seal and the seventh vial. Mountains typify kingdoms and governments; islands are symbolical of smaller and isolated governments. All will be affected. No doubt when the great earthquakes will shake the very foundations of the earth, many islands will also disappear.

Jasper. A precious stone, most likely our diamond. See exposition of chapter iv.

Jerusalem. The earthly and the heavenly Jerusalem are mentioned in the book. During the tribulation the earthly Jerusalem will be the seat of the Antichrist, the false Prophet. Jerusalem is for this reason called "Sodom and Egypt" (xi: 8). Then Jerusalem will pass through her worst history. A great siege will take place at the close of the tribulation period and the city will fall (Zech. xiv). After that Jerusalem will become the capital of the kingdom of Christ and a great temple will be erected, the universal place of worship during the millennium. The heavenly Jerusalem is above the earth. From there the glorious reign of Christ and the Saints will be executed. This glorious city will come down out of heaven at the end of the millennium to find its eternal resting place on the new earth. (Chapter xxi-xxii.)

Jezebel. Symbolical of the Papacy. The corruptress which claims to be the Bride of Christ, but plays the harlot. See chapters ii and xvii.

Judgment. Judgment falls upon the earth during the seven years, which constitute the end of the age. When the Lord comes in His glory the great judgment of the nations takes place. Chapter xix: 11, etc., compare with Matt. xxv: 31. After the millennium the second resurrection takes place and the great white throne judgment is the judgment of the wicked dead.

King of the Nations. xv: 2-4. King of the Saints should be changed (see margin) to King of the nations. Our Lord is the King of the nations, the King of kings

Lake of Fire. The place which God has prepared for the Devil and his angels. The Beast and the false prophet will be cast there; also the Assyrian, the King of the North, the nations who followed the Beast and all the wicked dead. Death and Hades will likewise be put into that place.

The Lamb. The Lamb (John i: 29), our Lord in His sacrificial character, is mentioned twenty-eight times in Revelation. The Lamb is worshipped by all. Thus we find the Song of the Lamb, the Throne of the Lamb and the Marriage of the Lamb, and the Wife of the Lamb (the church) in this book.

Lightning. Symbolical of the divine judgment Wrath.

Locust Army. Symbolical of the host of demons, which come out of the abyss to torment mankind.

Lord's Day, The. Mentioned but once in i: 10. It is the first day of the week on which John saw the great Patmos vision.

Man-child. Chapter xii. The Man-child is the Lord Jesus Christ.

Mark of the Beast. Some special mark which declares ownership. As the Holy Spirit seals those who trust on Christ, so Anti-christ will put his mark upon those who follow him.

Millennium, The. Millennium means "a thousand years." Six times this period of blessing and glory is mentioned in Rev. xx.

Moon as blood. The Moon is symbolical of derived authority. Blood is the symbol of death. Apostate Israel and the apostate church passing through the most severe judgments are symbolized by this figure.

Morning Star, The. Christ in His Coming for the church. Chapters xxii: 16; ii: 28.

Mountain. A kingdom.

Mountains, Seven. Rome is the city built upon the seven hills. See exposition of chapter xvii.

Nicolaitanes. Mentioned in the message of Ephesus and Pergamos. They signify the domineering, priestly class which assumed an unscriptural place of authority in the church.

Palms. Emblems of victory.

Rainbow. The symbol of covenant and of mercy. Mentioned twice. Around the Throne (chapter iv) and around His head (chapter x).

Rest of the Dead. xx: 5. Meaning those who had not part in the First Resurrection, hence the wicked dead.

River of Life. xxii: 1. Symbolical of the fullness of life, glory and blessing.

Saints. The Saints in Revelation include all the Saints. The Old and New Testament Saints are seen under the figure of the twenty-four elders. The suffering Saints are the Jewish Saints and the remnant of Israel, as well as the multitude of nations, who accept the final message and come out of the great tribulation. (Chapter vii.)

Satan. The entire book reveals his person, his work and his destiny. His work may be traced in the church-messages. Then we have his work during the tribulation and his final work after the millennium.

Scorpions. Symbolical of the torment caused by the army of demons under the fifth trumpet judgment.

Sea. Symbol of the nations. Also the literal sea, which gives up the dead. Then there will be no more sea. All wickedness and restlessness will cease forever.

Seven. The divine number. No other Book in the Bible contains so many "sevens" as this final Bible-book, the Revelation. There are seven angels, churches, attributes of the Lord, heads, horns, eyes, spirits, lamps, seals, trumpets, vials, plagues, stars, thunders, times and a sevenfold doxology.

Song. The songs of the Redeemed and the Song of Moses and the Lamb are mentioned in the Book.

Stars. See exposition on the meaning of the seven stars in His hand. Stars are also symbolical of lesser authorities, which will all fall during the tribulation period. Lights in the night.

Sun. The symbol of supreme authority.

Synagogue of Satan. Mentioned in the messages to Smyrna and Philadelphia. It means a Judaized Christianity as seen in Ritualistic, professing Christendom.

Temple. The tribulation temple is in view in chapter xi: 1-3. The millennial temple is seen in vii: 15. Then there is the temple in heaven. Chapter xvi: 17. In the heavenly Jerusalem there is no temple. xxi: 22.

Third Part. Mentioned in connection with men, the sea, the stars of heaven, the Sun and the Moon. It probably refers exclusively to the Roman empire, which in its different aspects and authorities, will be affected during these judgments.

Two horns. The Beast out of the land has two horns like a lamb, but speaks like the dragon. He is the counterfeit Christ.

Waters, Many. Symbolical of peoples and nations over which the Romish whore has authority.

White. Color of righteousness and purity; also denoting victorious conquests. We have in Revelation, white Robes, the white horses, white linen, a white cloud and a white Throne.

Witnesses. See in Rev. xi about the two witnesses.

Wrath. We read of the Wrath of God and the wrath of the Lamb. The wrath of God is completed with the pouring out of the vials. The wrath of the Lamb will be executed when He comes in Glory.

Zion. Mentioned only once in Rev., chapter xiv: 1. It means the literal Zion in Palestine. Upon that holy hill of Zion the glory will rest during the millennium. See Psalm cxxxii: 13-14.

APPENDIX III.

List of Corrections, in Readings and Renderings of Revelation.*

In ch. i. 2, for *"and of all things that he saw,"* read "as much as he saw." In ver. 5, for *"loved,"* read "loveth." In ver 6, for *"kings and priests,"* "a kingdom, even priests." At end, omit *"and ever."* In ver. 8, omit *"the beginning and the ending"*; it was probably inserted as an explanation of "Alpha and Omega." For *"the Lord,"* read "the Lord God." In ver. 9, omit *"who also am."* Omit *"Christ"* (twice). In ver. 11 omit *"I am Alpha and Omega, the first and the last: and."* The words *"which are in Asia,"* are wanting in all our MSS. of every date. In ver. 17, omit *"unto me."* In ver. 18, omit *"Amen."* In ver. 19, for *"write,"* "write therefore." In ver. 20, omit *"which thou sawest."*

In ch. ii. I, for *"of* Ephesus," read "in Ephesus." In ver. 3, for *"hast not been weary,"* "hast not fainted." In ver. 5, omit *"quickly."* In ver. 7, omit *"the midst*

---

* As suggested by Dean H. Alford.

of." In ver. 9, omit *"works, and."* In ver. 10, for "Fear *none of those things,"* "Fear not those things." In ver. 13, omit *"thy works and."* For *"my faithful martyr,"* read "my martyr, my faithful one." In ver. 15, for *"which thing 1 hate,"* read, *with all the MSS.,* "in like manner." In ver. 16, "Repent therefore." In ver. 17, omit *"to eat."* In ver. 20, for "I have *a few things* against thee, *because,"* read "I have against thee, that." For *"that woman,"* read "thy wife." For *"to teach and to seduce,"* "and she teacheth and seduceth." In ver. 21, for *"of her fornication; and she repented not,"* read "and she will not repent of her fornication." At end of ver. 22, for *"their* deeds," "her deeds." In ver. 24 (beginning), omit *"and."* And for "I *will* put," "I put."

In ch. iii. 2, for *"God,"* read "my God." In ver. 3, omit *"on thee"* (first time). In ver. 4, read *with all the MSS.,* "nevertheless thou hast," etc.; and on the same authority, omit *"even."* In ver. 7, for *"he that is holy, he that is true,"* read "the true one, the holy one." For *"shutteth,"* "shall shut." In ver. 11, omit *"Behold."* In ver. 14, for *"of the Laodiceans,"* read "in Laodicea." In ver. 16, for *"cold nor hot,"* "hot nor cold." In ver. 17, for *"wretched and miserable,"* "the wretched one and the pitiable one." In ver. 18, for *"anoint thine eyes with eye-salve,"* "eye-salve to anoint thine eyes."

In ch. iv. 4, for *"upon the seats I saw four-and-twenty elders,"* "upon the four and twenty thrones, elders"; omit *"they had."* In ver. 6, for *"there was,"* "as it were." In ver. 8 there is considerable confusion as to the number of times which the word "holy" is repeated. In the Sinaitic MS. it occurs eight times; in the later Vatican nine times; in other MSS. twice, or six times or eight. In the Alexandrine, and the old versions, there are considerable variations. We probably should read three times. In ver. 11, for *"O Lord,"* "our Lord and God;" and for *"are,"* "were."

In ch. v. 4, *"and to read"* must be omitted. In ver. 5, omit "to loose." In ver. 6, omit *"and lo."* In ver. 8, for *"harps,"* "an harp." In vers. 9 and 10 there is considerable variation. In ver. 9, *"us"* is omitted by the Alexandrine MS., and probably, from what follows, was not found originally in the text. In ver. 10, all the MSS. for "us," have *"them."* The Alexandrine MS. omits *"unto our God."* For *"kings and priests,"* read "a kingdom and priests" (the Sinaitic MS. has "a kingdom and priesthood"). For *"we shall reign,"* read "they reign." The reading of the English version rests on hardly any authority. In ver. 11, for *"the voice,"* the Sinaitic MS. and others have "as it were the voice." For the latter clause of ver. 14, read "and the elders fell down and worshipped;" omitting the rest. The Authorized Version has absolutely no authority.

In ch. vi: 1, for *"seals,"* read "seven seals" (the Sinaitic MS. has "seven," without *"seals"*). For *"as it were the noise of thunder, one of the four beasts saying,"* read "one of the four living-beings saying, as it were the noise of thunder." In the same verse, and in vers. 3, 5, 7, after the word "Come," omit *"and see."* In ver. 6, for *"a voice,"* read "as it were a voice." In ver. 11, for *"white robes were,"* "a white robe was." In ver. 12, omit *"lo";* and for *"the moon,"* "the whole moon," *i. e.,* "the full moon."

In ch. vii. 1, for *"these things,"* "this." From vers. 5 to 8, omit in every case except the first (Judah) and the last (Benjamin), the words *"were sealed."* In ver. 14, for *"Sir,"* "my lord."

In ch. viii. 7, omit *"angel";* and after the word, "earth," insert "and the third part of the earth was burnt up." In ver. 13, instead of *"an angel,"* read, with all the oldest MSS., "an eagle."

In ch. ix. 9, for *"battle,"* read "war." In ver. 13 the reading is very uncertain. We have but *two* ancient MSS. here; of these, the Alexandrine omits *"four,"* and the Sinaitic reads merely, "I heard the voice of the golden altar," etc. In ver. 18, for *"these three,"* read, with nearly all the authorities, "these three plagues." In ver. 19, for *"their power,"* read "the power of the horses." Curiously enough the Alexandrine MS. has for "horses," "places," but it is probably a mistake between two similar Greek words.

In ch. x. 4, *"had uttered their voices,"* "spoke." In ver. 5, for *"hand,"* "right-hand." In ver. 11, for *"he said,"* "they say."

Ch. xi. 1 should stand: "And there was given me a reed like unto a rod, saying." In ver. 4, for *"God,"* "Lord." In ver. 8, for *"bodies,"* "body," and for *"our Lord,"* "their Lord," or "the Lord." In ver. 9, for *"bodies,"* "body," and for *"shall see,"* *"shall not suffer,"* "look upon," and "suffer not." Also in ver.

10, for *"shall rejoice," "rejoice."* In ver. 15, for *"kingdoms of this world are become the kingdoms of our Lord,"* "kingdom over this world is become our Lord's." In ver. 17 omit *"and art to come."*

In ch. xii. 12, omit *"the inhabiters of."* In ver. 17, omit *"Christ."* The Sinaitic MS. has "God."

In ch. xiii. 1, for *"I stood......and saw......,"* read "he stood......and I saw." In ver. 6, for *"and them that dwell,"* read which dwell." In ver. 7, for *"all kindreds, and tongues, and nations,"* "every tribe, and people, and tongue, and nation." In ver. 10 there is great confusion. The Authorized Version has hardly any authority. The most probable reading, according to the most ancient MSS., is: "If any is for captivity, into captivity he goeth: if any to be slain with the sword, he must be slain with the sword." In ver. 13, omit *"from heaven."* In ver. 17, for "the mark," *or* the name," read "the mark, the name."

In ch. xiv., for *"a lamb,"* "the lamb." For *"his* Father's name," "his name and his Father's name." In ver. 2, for *"I heard the voice of harpers,"* "the noise which I heard was of harpers." In ver. 5, for *"for they are without fault before the throne of God,"* read only, "they are blameless." The words "before the throne of God" are inserted absolutely without any MS. authority. In ver. 8, for *"another angel,"* read "another second angel." After Babylon, insert "the Great." In ver. 9, for *"the third angel,"* read "another third angel." In ver. 12, for *"the saints: here are they that,"* "the saints, which." In ver. 13, omit *"unto me."* For *"and their works,"* "for their works." In ver. 15, omit *"for thee."*

In ch. xv. 2, omit *"and over his mark."* In ver. 3, for "King of *saints,"* read "King of the nations." The Paris MS. reads "King of the *ages." King of saints* has no authority whatever. In ver. 5, omit *"behold."*

In ch. xvi. 1, for *"vials,"* read "seven vials." In ver. 2, for *"upon* the earth," read "into the earth." In vers. 3, 4, omit *"angel";* and so throughout. In ver. 5, omit *"O Lord."* For *"and wast, and shalt be,"* read "and wast holy." The text of the Authorized Version is a pure invention, resting on no authority whatever. In ver. 6, omit "for" (second time). In ver. 7, for *"I heard another out of the altar say,"* "I heard the altar saying." The Authorized Version rests on only one MS., and that of the twelfth century. In ver. 14, omit the words *"earth and of the."* The name *"Armageddon"* is written (H)armagedon, with one *d,* in the ancient MSS. The aspirate is in the Hebrew name, and in many of our MSS. (the ancient ones not having any aspirates). In ver. 17, for *"into,"* "upon." Omit "of *heaven";* the Sinaitic MS. has *"of God,"* showing by the variety that the words were interpolated. In ver. 18, for *"since men were,"* "since there was a man."

In ch. xvii. 8, for *"yet is,"* read "shall come again." The Authorized Version has no MS. authority at all. The Sinaitic MS. reads, "and is present." In ver. 9, omit *"and."* In ver. 13, for *"shall* give," "give." In ver. 16, for *"which thou sawest upon the beast,"* read "which thou sawest, and the best."

In ch. xviii. 2, *"mightily"* has no MS. authority whatever for it. In ver 3, omit *"the wine of."* In ver. 13, after cinnamon, add, "and amomum" (a famous ointment made from an Asiatic shrub). The omission was probably occasioned by the similarity of readings of cinnamomum and amomum. In ver. 14, for *"departed,"* "perished"; and for *"thou shalt,"* "men shall." In ver. 17, for *"all the company in ships,"* "every one who saileth any whither." In ver. 20, for *"ye holy apostles,"* "ye saints and ye apostles."

In ch. xix. 1, for *"a great voice,"* "as it were a loud voice." For *"Salvation, and glory, and honour, and power, unto the Lord our God,"* "the salvation and the glory belong unto our God." In ver. 12, for *"he had a name written,"* "having names written." In ver. 15, for *"fierceness and wrath,"* "fierceness of the wrath." In ver. 17, for *"supper of the great God,"* "great banquet of God." In ver. 20, for *"and with him the false prophet,"* "and those that were with him, the false prophet."

In ch. xx. 9, omit *"from God."* In ver. 12, for *"small and great, stand before God,"* "the great and the small, standing before the throne." In ver. 14 it should stand, "This is the second death (even) the lake of fire."

In ch. xxi. 2, *"John"* is omitted by all MSS. whatever, and rests on no authority. In ver. 3, for *"heaven,"* read "the throne." In ver. 5, omit *"unto me."* In ver. 6, for *"It is done,"* "They are fulfilled." So the Alexandrine MS. The Sinaitic and many later MSS. have only, "I am become the Alpha," etc. In ver. 7, for *"all things,"* "these things." In ver. 10, for *"that great city, the holy Jerusalem,"* "the holy city, Jerusalem."

In ver. 14, for *"the names,"* "the twelve names." In ver. 15, for *"had a golden reed,"* "had for a measure a golden reed." In ver. 24, omit *"of them that are saved";* and also omit *"and honour."*

In ch. xxii. 1, omit *"pure."* In ver. 5, for *"no night there,"* "no more night." In ver. 6, for *"of the holy prophets,"* "of the spirits of the prophets." In ver. 7, for *"Behold,"* "and behold"; so also in ver. 12. In ver. 11, for *"be righteous still,"* "still do righteousness." In ver. 12, for *"shall be,"* "is." In ver. 14, for *"do his commandments,"* which is the reading of the later MSS., "wash their robes," which is that of the more ancient. The variety is curious. The two clauses in the Greek sound exceedingly like one another, and hence the mistake. In such a case we are bound to follow the more ancient evidence. In ver. 17, put a semicolon at "come" (third time), and omit *"and"* before "whosoever." In ver. 18, omit *"For."* For *"these things,"* read "them." In ver. 19, for "the *book* of life," read "the tree of life." Omit *"and from the things."* The last verse should be: "The grace of the Lord Jesus be with the saints. Amen." So the Sinaitic MS. The Alexandrine reads, "be with all" (and no more). The later MSS. read "be with all the saints." But no MS. whatever reads as the Authorized Version.

This most numerous crop of corrigenda in the readings is matched by an equally numerous one as regards the renderings. By no book has the Church in this land acted so unfaithfully as by this. She has given her members an incorrect version of it, in part of human invention, and she has repudiated the blessing pronounced (ch. i. 3) on its public reading.

It is impossible to give the corrigenda in rendering at the same length as we have hitherto done. They occur at every turn.

In ch. i. 2, for *"bare record of the word of God and of the,"* "testified the word of God and the testimony of the." In ver. 7, for *"clouds,"* "the clouds"; and for *"kindred,"* "the tribes." In ver. 19, for *"hast seen,"* "sawest"; for *"and the things which are,"* and what things they are"; and for *"hereafter,"* "after these."

In ch. ii. 4, for *"I have somewhat against thee, because......,"* substitute "I have against thee, that ......" In ver. 8, for *"is alive,"* "revived." Put a semicolon at "poverty," and proceed, removing the parenthesis, "nevertheless thou art rich." In ver. 13, for *"seat,"* "throne." For *"hast not denied my faith,"* "didst not deny the faith of me." In ver. 22, for *"will cast,"* "cast." In ver. 27, for *"receive as I receive,"* "as I also have received."

In ch. iii. 2, for *"are ready,"* "were ready." In ver. 5, for *"but,"* "and." In ver. 8, for *"for thou hast a little strength and hast kept my word and hast not denied,"* "because thou hast little power, and thou didst keep my word and didst not deny." In ver. 10, "didst keep," and "is about to come." In ver. 16, for *"I will spue thee,"* "I shall soon spue thee." In ver. 17, "knowest not that thou of all others are the wretched one and the pitiable one, and poor," etc. In ver. 18, for *"trial in the fire,"* "fresh-smelted from the fire." In ver. 21, for *"am set,"* "sat."

In ch. iv: 1, for "a door *was opened,"* "a door set open." For *"the first voice which I heard was of,"* etc., "the former voice which I heard as of," etc. **Not** the first voice after the vision, but the *former voice,* which spoke with him before, is meant. In verse 2, for *"a throne was set in heaven and one sat,"* "a throne was there in heaven, and one sitting." In verse 4, for *"seats,"* "thrones." The word is the same throughout: and the translators had no right to vary it, especially after our Lord's prophecy, Matt. xix: 28. In verse 6 and henceforward, the unhappy translation *"beasts"* should by all means be corrected. The original word is "living beings," which might well be retained, sometimes calling them merely "beings" where they are mentioned several times together. In verse 7, *"calf"* should be "steer." It is a young bullock, not a mere calf, that is meant. In verse 8, for *"and they were full of eyes within,"* "around and within they are full of eyes." In verse 9, for *"sat,"* "sitteth." In verse 10, for *"fall,"* "shall fall"; and for *"worship,"* "shall worship"; and for *"cast,"* "shall cast." In verse 11, for *"glory and honour and power,"* "the glory and the honour and the might," and for *"hast created,"* "didst create."

In chapter v: 1, for *"in* the right hand," "on the right hand." The hand was open, and the book lying on it. In verse 3, for "no *man,"* "no one." In verse 5, for *"hath prevailed to,"* "conquered, so as to." In verse 6, for *"stood a Lamb as it had been slain,"* "a Lamb standing as if slain." In verse 8, for *"had taken,"* "took"; and for *"saints,"* "the saints." In verse 9, for *"sung,"* "sing." In verse 12, for *"was slain,"* "hath been slain"; and for *"power,"* "the power." In verse 13, for *"such as are in the sea,"* "upon the sea." For *"saying,"* "all saying."

In chapter vi: 2, for *"to* conquer," which looks as if it were merely prophetic of the future, "in order that he might," or "in order to, conquer." In verse 3, omit *"had";* and so in verses 5, 7, 9, 12. In verse 8, for *"Hell,"* substitute "Hades"; Hell is the place of punishment, as now understood, whereas the abode of the departed is here meant. In verse 9, for *"were,"* "have been." For *"held,"* "bore." In verse 10, for *"O Lord,"* "Thou Master." In verse 14, for *"departed,"* "parted asunder." In verse 16, for *"said,"* "say." In verse 17, for *"shall be,"* "is."

In chapter vii: 2, for *"ascending from the east,"* "coming up from the rising of the sun." In verse 9, for "no *man,"* "no one." In verse 12, before "blessing," and each of the substantives following, insert "the." In verse 14, for *"came out of great,"* "come out of the great." For *"have washed,"* "they washed." In verse 15, for *"shall dwell among them,"* "shall spread his habitation over them"; literally, "shall tabernacle upon them." It is very difficult to express the glorious image; but the Authorized Version is wretchedly short of any rendering of it. In verse 17, *"feed"* is "tend," or "shepherd." It does not imply the giving of food, but the leading and pasturing.

In chapter viii: 2, for *"stood,"* "stand." In verse 3, for *"at,"* "over." Verse 4 should stand: "And the smoke of the incense ascended up to the prayers of the saints out of the angel's hand before God." In verse 12, for *"likewise,"* "in like manner." In verse 13, for *"yet to sound,"* "about to sound."

In chapter ix: 1, for *"fall,"* "fallen." For *"the bottomless pit,"* "the pit of the abyss," *i. e.,* of hell. So also in verse 2. In verse 6, for *"desire,"* "vehemently desire." In verse 7, for *"unto battle,"* "for war." In verse 14, for *"in,"* "on." In verse 15, for *"for an hour, and a day, and a month, and a year,"* "against the hour, and the day, and the month, and the year." In verse 17, for *"of fire and of jacinth, and brimstone,"* "red as fire, and blue as smoke, and yellow as brimstone."

In chapter x: 1, for *"a* rainbow," "the rainbow." In verse 3, for *"seven thunders,"* "the seven thunders." In verse 6, for *"that there should be time no longer,"* substitute "that there shall be delay no longer." In verse 7, for *"when He shall begin to sound,"* "when He shall be about to sound." For *"declared,"* "declared the glad tidings," "evangelized." In verse 10, for *"was bitter,"* "was embittered." Verse 11 should run ". . . . . .again concerning people, and nations, and tongues, and many kings."

In chapter xi: 2, for *"leave out,"* "cast thou out"; for *"is given,"* "was given." In verse 5 (twice), for *"will hurt them,"* "is minded to hurt them." In verse 6, for *"the bottomless pit,"* "the abyss." In verse 9, for *"they of the people and kindreds,"* "some from among the people and tribes"; for *"shall see,"* "look upon"; and for *"graves,"* "a tomb." In verse 11 for *"three,"* "the three." In verse 12, for *"a cloud,"* "the clouds." In verse 16, for *"seats,"* "thrones." In verse 18, for *"reward,"* "their reward." In verse 19, for *"testament,"* "covenant."

In chapter xii: 2, for *"cried,"* "crieth." In verse 3, *"crowns"* were better "diadems": it is not the usual word (*stephanous*), but *diademata.* In verse 4, for *"drew,"* "draweth" [down]; for *"stood,"* "standeth." End the verse, "which is ready to be delivered, that when she hath borne, he may devour her child." In verse 5, for *"who was to rule,"* "which shall rule." In verse 10, for *"salvation and strength,"* "the salvation and the might." For *"accused,"* "accuseth." In verse 11, for *"by the blood......,"* *"by the word,"* "because of the blood,".......because of the word." In verse 14, for *"a great eagle,"* "the great eagle." In verse 15 (twice), for *"flood,"* "river"; and so in verse 16. In verse 17, for *"went,"* "departed."

In chapter xiii: 1, for *"beast,"* "wild beast"; and so in verse 2, 11. The same word is used afterwards, but it need not be marked any further. *"Crowns,"* again, is "diadems." In verse 4, for *"which,"* "because he." In verse 5, for *"to continue,"* "to work." In verse 6, for *"in blasphemy,"* "for blasphemies." In verse 14, *"which he had power to do,"* "which it was given him to work." In verse 15, for *"he had power,"* "it was given him"; for *"life,"* "breath"; for *"both,"* "even."

In chapter xiv: 3, for *"beasts,"* "living creatures." For *"no man,"* "no one"; and for *"were redeemed,"* "have been purchased." In verse 4, for *"redeemed,"* "purchased." For *"being the first fruits,"* "as a first fruit." In verse 6, for *"kindred,"* "tribe." In verse 8, for *"because she made,"* "which hath made." In verse 13, for *"follow them,"* "follow with them."

In chapter xv: 1, for *"the seven last plagues, for,"* "seven plagues, which are the last, because." In verse 2, for *"the* harps," "harps." In verse 7, for *"beasts,"* "living creatures."

In chapter xvi: 3, for *"as the blood of a dead man,"* "blood, as of a dead man." In verse 8, for *"have shed,"* "shed." In verse 10, for *"seat,"* "throne." For *"was full of darkness,"* "became darkened." In verse 12, for *"the kings of the east,"* "the kings which come from the rising of the sun." In verse 14, for *"spirits of devils,"* "the spirits of demons." In verse 14, for *"battle,"* "war." In verse 16, for *"great Babylon,"* "Babylon the great."

In chapter xvii: 2, for *"have committed,"* "committed"; and for *"have been made,"* "were made." In verse 3, for *"beast,"* "wild beast." In verse 5, for *"harlots,"* "the harlots"; and for *"abominations,"* "the abominations." In verse 6, for *"martyrs,"* "witnesses." In verse 8, for *"bottomless pit,"* "abyss." For "shall go," "goeth." In verse 10, for *"there are,"* "they are"; and continue, "the five are fallen, the one is," etc. In verse 17, for *"hath* put," "put."

In chapter xviii: 1, for *"come* down," "coming down." In verse 2, for *"devils,"* "demons." In verse 3, for *"have* committed," "committed"; and for *"are* waxed," "waxed." In verse 6, for *"hath filled, fill,"* "mixed, mix." In verse 8, for *"hath judged,"* "judgeth." In verse 9, for *"have* committed," "committed." In verse 11, omit *"shall."* In verse 12, for *"thyine,"* "citron." For *"all manner vessels,"* "every article" (twice). In verse 13, for *"souls,"* "persons." In verse 14, for *"the fruits that thy soul lusted after are,"* "the harvest of the desire of thy soul is." For *"all things which were dainty and goodly,"* "all thy fat things and thy splendid things." In verse 16, for *"decked,"* "gilded." In verse 17, for *"come to nought,"* "made desolate." For *"shipmaster,"* "pilot." In verse 18, for *"what city,"* "who"; and for *"this,"* "the." In verse 19, for *"that,"* "the"; *"wherein,"* "whereby." In verse 20, for *"hath avenged her,"* "hath judged your judgment." In verse 21, for *"a mighty angel,"* "one strong angel." In verse 24, for *"were slain,"* "have been slain."

In chapter xix: 3, for *"rose up,"* "goeth up." In verse 4, for *"beasts,"* "living-creatures"; for *"sat,"* "sitteth." In verse 8, for *"clean and white,"* "bright and pure"; for *"fine linen,"* "the fine linen"; for "saints," "the saints." In verse 11, for *"sat,"* "sitteth." In verse 12, for *"crowns,"* "diadems." In verse 19, for *"beast,"* "wild beast"; for *"war,"* "their war"; for *"sat,"* "sitteth."

In chapter xx: 1, for *"bottomless pit,"* "abyss"; so also in verse 2. In verse 4, for *"hands,"* "hand." In verse 11, for *"sat,"* "sitteth." In verse 12, for *"the books,"* "books." In verse 13, for *"hell,"* "Hades"; so also in verse 14.

In chapter xxi: 1, for *"there was no more sea,"* "the sea is no more." In verse 4, for *"all tears,"* "every tear." In verse 5, for *"sat,"* "sitteth." In verse 7, "I will be to him a God, and he shall be to me a son." In verse 8, for *"whoremongers,"* "fornicators." In verse 9, for *"full,"* "and were full." In verse

15, for *"foundations,"* "foundation-stones." In verse 24, for "in the light," "by means of the light." In verse 27, for *"worketh abomination, or maketh a lie,"* "worketh abomination or falsehood"; for *"they,"* "only they."

In chapter xxii: 5, for *"giveth them light,"* "shall shine upon them." In verses 8, 9, read "I John am he who heard these things, and saw them. And when I heard and saw," etc. In verse 11, for *"let him be holy still,"* "let him sanctify himself still." In verse 14, for *"right to,"* "power over." In verse 15, prefix "the" to each of the classes enumerated. In verse 16, for *"have sent,"* "sent"; for *"and the bright and morning star,"* "and bright morning star." In verse 20, omit *"even so."*

THE END